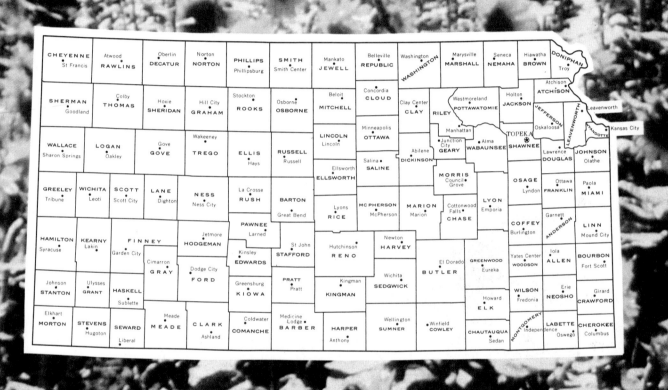

The New
Enchantment of America

KANSAS

By Allan Carpenter

CHILDRENS PRESS, CHICAGO

ACKNOWLEDGMENTS

For assistance in the preparation of the revised edition, the author thanks:
RON WELCH, Publications Division, Kansas Department of Economic Development.

American Airlines—Anne Vitaliano, Director of Public Relations; *Capitol Historical Society*, Washington, D. C.; *Newberry Library,* Chicago, Dr. Lawrence Towner, Director; *Northwestern University Library*, Evanston, Illinois; *United Airlines*—John P. Grember, Manager of Special Promotions; Joseph P. Hopkins, Manager, News Bureau; Carl Provorse, *Carpenter Publishing House.*

UNITED STATES GOVERNMENT AGENCIES: *Department of Agriculture*—Robert Hailstock, Jr., Photography Division, Office of Communication; Donald C. Schuhart, Information Division, Soil Conservation Service. *Army*—Doran Topolosky, Public Affairs Office, Chief of Engineers, Corps of Engineers. *Department of Interior*—Louis Churchville, Director of Communications; EROS Space Program—Phillis Wiepking, Community Affairs; Charles Withington, Geologist; Mrs. Ruth Herbert, Information Specialist; Bureau of Reclamation; National Park Service—Fred Bell and the individual sites; Fish and Wildlife Service—Bob Hines, Public Affairs Office. *Library of Congress*—Dr. Alan Fern, Director of the Department of Research; Sara Wallace, Director of Publications; Dr. Walter W. Ristow, Chief, Geography and Map Division; Herbert Sandborn, Exhibits Officer. *National Archives*—Dr. James B. Rhoads, Archivist of the United States; Albert Meisel, Assistant Archivist for Educational Programs; David Eggenberger, Publications Director; Bill Leary, Still Picture Reference; James Moore, Audio-Visual Archives. *United States Postal Service*—Herb Harris, Stamps Division.

For assistance in the preparation of the first edition, the author thanks:
Nyle H. Miller, Secretary, Kansas State Historical Society; Ken Johnson, Administrative Assistant to the Governor; and Jack Lacy, Director, State of Kansas Department of Economic Development.

Illustrations on the preceding pages:
Cover photograph: Front Street, Boot Hill Museum, Inc., Dodge City, Kansas
Page 1: Commemorative stamps of historic interest
Pages 2-3: State flower blankets the countryside, USDA, Robert Hailstock, Jr.
Page 3: (Map) USDI Geological Survey
Pages 4-5: Kansas City area, EROS Space Photo, USDI Geological Survey, EROS Data Center

Project Editor, Revised Edition:
   Joan Downing
Assistant Editor, Revised Edition:
   Mary Reidy

Library of Congress Cataloging in Publication Data

Carpenter, Allan, 1917-
   Kansas.

   (His The new enchantment of America)
   SUMMARY: Discusses the history and geography of the state as well as famous citizens and interesting sites.
   1. Kansas—Juvenile literature.
[1. Kansas] I. Title. II. Series.
F681.3.C3   1979   978.1   79-12442
ISBN 0-516-04116-9

Contents

A TRUE STORY TO SET THE SCENE 9
A Chorus of Praise

LAY OF THE LAND.. 11
What Kansas Is Like Today—Kansas in Times Past

FOOTSTEPS ON THE LAND................................. 17
The Earliest Kansans—Explorers—Settlers and Trailblazers—Growing Pains

YESTERDAY AND TODAY 29
Kansas and the Civil War—Frontier Cow Towns—Life on the Prairie—Biggest Powwow in History—From the Halls of Congress to the Shores of Aguinaldo—A Fresh New Century

NATURAL TREASURES 43

PEOPLE USE THEIR TREASURES 49
Nation's Breadbasket—Industry—Mineral Production—Transportation—Newspapers

HUMAN TREASURES.. 59
Five Stars—Other Public Figures—Seasoned with Sage—Skies Are Not Cloudy All Day: Art, Music, Literature—Hero in the Philippines—Such Interesting People

TEACHING AND LEARNING................................ 67

ENCHANTMENT OF KANSAS.............................. 69
The Northeast—The Southeast—Central Kansas—Where the West Is Tamed—Dodge City, The Wild West

HANDY REFERENCE SECTION 87
Instant Facts—You Have a Date with History—Thinkers, Doers, Fighters—Governors of the State of Kansas

INDEX... 91

PICTURE CREDITS... 96

ABOUT THE AUTHOR 96

When H.M. Carl Gustaf XVI of Sweden visited the United States in 1976, one of the highlights of his tour was the performance of the Messiah *at Bethany College, Lindsborg. The huge audience, mammoth choir, and large orchestra are shown on this occasion listening to the welcoming speech to the king by Swedish ambassador to the United States, Count Wilhem Wachtmeister.*

A True Story to Set the Scene

A CHORUS OF PRAISE

"Hallelujah, Hallelujah, Hallelujah!" The voices resounded; the organ pealed forth; the orchestra swelled with ever-increasing volume. As Handel's honored classic reached its great climax, the audience stood silently, thrilled, as audiences all over the world had been for more than a hundred years, to hear a performance of the *Messiah*.

But this was not one of the great concert halls of Europe, not one of the famed choruses of London or Rome. The beloved music was being sung so close to nearby wheat fields that it might have been heard there. These fields were green and rippling with the promise of renewed life.

This was Kansas, a Kansas still in its pioneer days, and that performance of the *Messiah* was one of the most remarkable in the history of music—one of the many accomplishments that mark the enchantment of Kansas

In 1878, when Dr. Carl Swensson and his bride, Alma, came to Lindsborg, Kansas, where he was to be pastor of Bethany church, they brought with them unusual ambitions for that small Swedish community in the heart of the growing state. More important, most of those ambitions would be realized.

The Swenssons loved music, as did most of their Swedish congregation, friends, and neighbors. They wanted to start a chorus. But this was not to be a chorus to sing only the lovely Swedish hymns and anthems. This chorus was created just for the purpose of presenting one of the greatest and most difficult musical works yet composed—Handel's magnificent oratorio the *Messiah*.

The Swenssons began the project in 1881. Their singers were eager but untrained; most of them had never seen a musical score. Those who lived far out on the prairie had to travel for as long as three hours by buggy, wagon, horseback, or on foot to attend a rehearsal.

Even mighty Chicago, with its newly formed Apollo Musical Club, had only recently begun to give concert performances of the

Messiah, and Chicago did not yet have a symphony orchestra. How could a small Swedish town on the Kansas prairies perform a feat that was difficult even in long-established centers of culture?

Yet the Kansans persisted, with inspired leadership and the kind of determination that overcomes all obstacles, and they succeeded beyond everyone's greatest hopes. They began a yearly tradition that has grown into one of the renowned musical festivals of the world—still in the midst of the Kansas wheat fields.

According to the magazine *Musical America,* "Away out in Kansas, on the edge of the prairie, there is an annual festival that means more to the musical growth of the United States than any production ever given in the opera houses of New York, Philadelphia, or Chicago."

All this was in the future, however, as the good people of Lindsborg and the surrounding area gathered in Bethany church that Easter Sunday of March 28, 1882.

Seventy-five well-rehearsed singers rose to begin the performance. A nineteen-piece orchestra, brought from Augustana College in Illinois, had just completed its tuning. One of the founders of Lindsborg, the Reverend Olof Olsson, was at the organ. Professor Joseph Osborn of Augustana College, the conductor, raised his baton and an outstanding performance began.

Mrs. Alma Swensson sang the soprano solo part, and Miss Anna Swensson was contralto.

As the hushed audience listened to their own Anna Swensson sing the beautiful "He Shall Feed His Flock Like a Shepherd," many of them must have thought of their own well-fed flocks, some within sound of the singers, and of the fields outside, green with the promise of spring. One of them expressed his feelings: "It's more than just some words from the Old Testament. It's the way we feel around here about the way the Lord has taken care of us."

Today, many throughout Kansas would still echo that sentiment.

Lay of the Land

WHAT KANSAS IS LIKE TODAY

If you were to buy a lot or farm anywhere in North America, or if you tried to locate your position on this continent according to latitude or longitude, Kansas would become very important. A point in Kansas would be vital to you even in such a simple matter as having your lot surveyed to be sure you hadn't gone over onto your neighbor's property when putting up a fence.

This is true because a point about eighteen miles (twenty-nine kilometers) southeast of Osborne is the geodetic center of the forty-eight conterminous United States and is accepted by other countries of North America. That is, every calculation of latitude or longitude or survey on the continent uses this point as its base.

Surveys or calculations in Kansas itself would show that the state can be divided into three different regions. The eastern third contains the Bluestem Belt (because of its bluestem grass) or the Flint Hills region; the Central Plains occupies the center; and the High Plains approximately the western third of the state.

Below: The Flint Hills region, or Bluestem Belt, of Kansas

All of Kansas is tilted like an old cellar door. It rises from about 700 feet (213 meters) in the southeast to more than 4,000 feet (1,219 meters) on the western border.

Although there are no mountains, Kansas has some unusual geological features. The Chalk Pyramids, between Oakley and Scott City, are rock formations that resemble the pyramids of ancient Egypt. There is even a chalk rock called the Sphinx because of its similarity to another Egyptian landmark. Rock City, near Minneapolis, is made up of about two hundred unusual sandstone formations, some of them almost perfect spheres, carved by wind and water. These are said to be unique in the world. The Gypsum Hills, near Medicine Lodge, are red stone mesas capped with white gypsum.

The basins are another unusual natural feature of Kansas. They are formed by the collapse of underground caves. When water erodes most of the limestone beneath the ground, the surface tumbles down and makes a deep depression in the earth. The Big Basin, in Clark County, is 1 mile (1.6 kilometers) long and 100 feet (30.5 meters) deep. Many of these basins are ancient, but others are being created continuously. In 1937, a farmer near Potwin noticed that a part of his farm was sinking; before another day had passed, a stretch of land 300 feet (91 meters) long and 250 feet (76 meters) wide had sunk and was filled with water.

Most people who are not familiar with the state probably would be surprised that Kansas can boast of six streams listed among the principal rivers of the United States by the U.S. Geological Survey. These are the Kansas, Republican, Smoky Hill, Arkansas, Cimarron, and Neosho. Other important rivers are the Blue, Solomon, Saline, Verdigris, and Marais des Cygnes.

Few man-made changes are more apparent than those that have transformed Kansas into a land of lakes. Kanopolis Dam on the Smoky Hill River is almost 3 miles (5 kilometers) long and 131 feet (40 meters) high. Cedar Bluff Dam is 12,500 feet (3,810 meters) long, and Tuttle Creek Dam, near Manhattan, is one of the largest earthen dams in the nation. These and other large dams were created by the federal government to provide lakes for water, to control

*Among the unusual geological features in Kansas are
Mushroom Rocks (above) and Monument Rocks (below).*

Lake Wilson

floods, and to bring beauty and recreation to large areas. There are also more than fifty natural lakes in Kansas.

The rain and snowfall that provide the water for these lakes come in widely different amounts to the eastern and the western parts of the state. Southeast Kansas receives 40 inches (102 centimeters) of precipitation a year, while the western edge has only about 16 inches (41 centimeters). Fortunately, 75 percent of this moisture comes during the growing season, when it is needed most.

KANSAS IN TIMES PAST

It hardly seems possible that this high and generally arid region was ever damp or cold, but many millions of years ago successive sea waters covered the state, ebbed away, and returned possibly as many as fifty times. At some age in the past, great quantities of water flowed down ancient rivers that originated in the Rocky Mountains. Tremendous amounts of sand, gravel, and rocks were carried down from the mountains and deposited in what is called the Great Plains region. The material brought by these ancient rivers makes up the surface of much of western Kansas.

A million years ago a great sheet of ice, a glacier, also covered a portion of northern Kansas. This was the only Ice Age glacier to reach Kansas, but it caused many changes. It brought in wonderful rich topsoil in great quantities. The sand and gravel deposits have been useful in construction, and the glacier leveled large areas, making them more suitable for farming. Nemaha and Brown counties, the site of the greatest glacial activity, are among the best farming counties in the state.

The past history of the land is illustrated in many areas where the older rocks have been exposed by digging or erosion. Also exposed are the fossil remains of many ancient creatures. In fact, Kansas is one of the finest sources of fossil remains. The largest beds of fossil crabs and other crustaceans are located in Kansas. A skeleton of the earliest ancestor of the horse was found in western Kansas. This tiny creature was only about 1 foot (.3 meter) high. Remains of toothed birds, huge turtles, and many other kinds of reptiles have been unearthed.

All of these creatures, of course, had become extinct long before the European settlers came to the area. How little they really knew in early times about the lay of the land in Kansas! Even a brilliant man such as Washington Irving could write: "Kansas must remain as uninhabitable as the deserts of Arabia." Another "expert" wrote: "Kansas is too isolated to become the abode of civilized man."

The story of how wrong they were is the story of Kansas.

Frederic Remington's famous painting of the Coronado expedition.

Footsteps on the Land

THE EARLIEST KANSANS

One by one, as the diggers worked, there came to light a hundred and forty bodies, neatly laid in carefully patterned rows. Many of the men were well over 6 feet (1.8 meters) tall. Was this a race of prehistoric giants? No one knows. This ancient burial site was discovered near Salina in 1937. Although it is one of the most important archaeological discoveries in the country, most of the facts about the people buried there still remain unknown.

Archaeologists and amateur diggers have found numerous artifacts used by the people who lived in the Kansas region before historic records were kept. Flint tools, fireplaces, bones, a very small amount of pottery, some picture writings on rocks and caves, and small mounds of earth remind us that people have lived in the Kansas area since the Stone Age.

Yet surprisingly little is known about the prehistoric residents. Apparently the earliest occupants of the Kansas region had civilizations that were poorly developed by contemporary standards.

EXPLORERS

Only fifty years after Columbus reached North America, the first Europeans were crossing Kansas. In 1541, a Spanish general, Francisco Vasquez de Coronado, entered what is now Kansas and went as far as the present site of Dodge City, then turned north and east and reached the region of present-day Junction City before turning back.

When the Spaniards failed to find the rich golden cities they thought were closer to Mexico, they pushed north into Kansas, because they had heard of a wealthy land called Quivira where there might be great riches of gold, silver, and jewels. Of course, there were no fabled cities in Kansas or any wise and wealthy civilizations. Quivira was nothing more than the land of the Wichita tribe.

Coronado returned to Mexico City in disgrace and died soon afterward. Although he found no gold and silver in Kansas, he admired the country. Coronado wrote to the king of Spain: "The soil itself is the most suitable that has been found for growing all the products of Spain, for besides being rich and black, it is well watered by arroyos, springs, and rivers." Europeans were to wait more than three centuries before discovering the real wealth of this "well-watered" land.

Another comment of Coronado is interesting; he wrote: "The plains are full of crooked necked oxen," about as vivid a description as ever was written of the buffalo.

Accompanying Coronado on his journey was a Franciscan priest, Father Juan de Padilla. He returned to what we now call Kansas after Coronado left. Father Padilla was soon killed by Indians, perhaps in 1542 in present-day central Kansas. And so, almost at the beginning of its history, Kansas witnessed the first Christian martyrdom in what became the United States.

Because of Coronado's explorations, the Spanish laid claim to the plains land of America, but the disappointed explorer left an even more interesting legacy. Coronado introduced the horse to the plains, and from that time on, the number of horses grew and the lives of the Indians were never the same. For more than 250 years, the Indians developed their horsemanship and depended on their horses without interference from the Europeans.

Several other explorers and traders found their way into the territory. Spain continued to claim control, and so did the French. In 1719, the French explorer Claude du Tisne crossed the southeastern corner of what is now Kansas. But at the same time that the civilizations of Spain, England, and France were developing in Mexico, Florida, the eastern American colonies, and Canada, the Kansas region received little attention.

Early explorers found a number of Indian tribes living in the place we call Kansas today. One of those tribes was the Kansa, or Kaw, Indians. Their tribal name means "people of the south wind," and so Kansas takes its name from an ancient Indian tribe. Other tribes living in Kansas included the Osage, Wichita, and Pawnee. The Osage were said to be "the tallest Indians in North America."

The Kansas Indians left their earth lodges and their villages to go

One of the earlier Kansa chiefs was White Plume (left), who was the great-great-grandfather of Charles Curtis, a vice president of the United States.

on great buffalo hunts, and the women did some farming, but mostly they fought each other. The greatest warriors were given the highest positions and the most respect. Only those who could prove that they had slain seven enemies in battle were given the high honor of having their chests tattooed.

The valley of the Walnut River has been called "the scene of more tribal conflicts than any other spot in America." Particularly fierce death struggles took place there between the Pawnee and their enemies, the Cheyenne. Only at Medicine Lodge, where all were under the protection of the Great Spirit, was there no fighting.

As the Europeans took over more and more Indian land in the East, many of the displaced Indians were provided escorts by the American government to find new lands in the West. As the eastern Indians arrived, many midwestern tribes moved farther west.

There is a fascinating story about one of the first displaced tribes. In the middle 1600s, members of the Picurie tribe fled from New Mexico to escape persecution by the Spaniards. They built an adobe village in present-day Scott County, known today as El Quartelejo. The buildings contain possibly the first hard walls built in Kansas. The mystery of what happened to their builders has never been solved.

The growing dislocation of the Indians was described dramatically by a Kansa chief, Al-le-ga-wa-hu, who declared, "Be-che-go, great father, you treat my people like a flock of turkeys. You come into our dwelling places and scare us out. We fly over and alight on another stream, but no sooner do we get well settled than again you

Prairie Fire, *a painting by George Catlin, is an indication of the long history of devastating fires in the Great Plains region.*

come along and drive us farther and farther. Ere long we shall find ourselves across the great Bah-do-Tunga [mountains] landing in the Ne-sah-tunga [ocean]."

In a few cases, the Indians protected their rights or received a fairer settlement when they seemed to have been cheated. Many of the Wyandots, who came from Ohio and founded part of present-day Kansas City, demanded and were granted American citizenship. They then sold their property in Kansas. Much later, greedy interests persuaded Congress to authorize the sale of the Wyandot tribal burial grounds in the heart of Kansas City, although these had been guaranteed forever. Public opinion soon encouraged delaying suits in courts, and Wyandot graves still remain in what is now a city park.

The history of Kansas really began to unfold in 1803 with the purchase of Louisiana Territory, including most of what is now Kansas, by the United States. President Thomas Jefferson sent Meriwether Lewis and William Clark to explore this new territory. The Lewis and Clark party viewed the Missouri River shores of Kansas as it reached the mouth of the Kansas River, at present-day Kansas City, on June 26, 1804. While passing along the Kansas border, they celebrated the Fourth of July in present Atchison County by shooting one of their heavy guns. At the mouth of the Nodaway River, some of the expedition members suffered sunstroke from the extreme heat. Shortly thereafter, the party passed Kansas and headed north to Nebraska.

Other explorers, however, soon followed and gave more careful attention to the state. In 1806, Lieutenant Zebulon Pike made his well-known trip, which included traveling the length of Kansas. Not long after beginning the overland journey into Kansas, Pike made this note: "My feet were blistered and very sore. I stood on a hill and in one view below me saw buffalo, elk, deer, cabrie [antelope] and panthers. . . . I prevented the men shooting at the game, not merely because of the scarcity of ammunition, but, as I conceived, the laws of morality forbade it also."

Later, in Pike's own words, his party held a "grand council with the Pawnees at which were present not less than 400 warriors. . . . Amongst the various demands and charges I gave them was that the

21

Council Grove, Pawnee Indian Council, *by Samuel Seymour,*
1819, shows the Zebulon Pike party with a large group of Pawnee at the
time the Spanish flag was exchanged for the American flag. This
was the first record of the American flag in the Kansas territory.

Spanish flag should be delivered to me and one of the United States'
flags be received and hoisted in its place, adding that they must
either be the children of the Spaniards or acknowledge their American Father. After a silence of some time, an old man rose, went to
the door, and took down the Spanish flag and brought it and laid it at
my feet, and then received the American flag and elevated it on the
staff which had lately borne the standard of his Catholic Majesty.''
This was the first record of the American flag in the Kansas territory.
The exact location of this incident is not known, but it is generally
thought to have occurred in Republic County.

22

SETTLERS AND TRAILBLAZERS

In 1824, the Reverend Benton Pixley set up a Christian mission among the Osage Indians in what is now Neosho County, west of Shaw. Within the next decades, the eastern prairie of Kansas was "dotted with mission stations of many denominations." The Shawnee Methodist Mission was begun in 1830 in Wyandotte County and was removed in 1839 to what is now Johnson County. The first Jesuit mission was established at Kickapoo in 1836. The Reverend and Mrs. Jotham Meeker opened a Baptist mission to the Ottawa Indians at Ottawa in 1837.

Early merchants were interested in Kansas, not as a site for business but as a possible cross-country route for shipping goods to the rich Spanish town of Santa Fe, where the people were eager to buy merchandise.

Even before the Indians gave their permission to use the route, Captain W.H. Becknell started out in 1822 with the first wagon party ever to attempt the overland route. Their experiences proved exciting: buffalo stampeded their horses; they were attacked by the Osage Indians; and, of course, they lost their way. Only a dry bed of sand greeted them where they expected to find the Cimarron River. Becknell did not know that during certain periods the river sank into its sandy bed and flowed underground.

While the party was suffering from extreme thirst, a tough old buffalo came along the dry river bed. The travelers reasoned that there had to be a source of water in the vicinity. Using their last energy, some of the men went on for several miles and found a water hole above ground. The expedition made the rest of the way to Santa Fe with little trouble.

Between 1825 and 1827, the United States government surveyed the Santa Fe Trail, and wagon trains began to use it regularly. The trail's largest section, nearly five hundred miles (eight hundred kilometers), was situated in present-day Kansas. Most of the trail parties took a longer route than the Becknell group to be sure of finding adequate amounts of drinking water.

The romance and adventure of the old Santa Fe Trail have been told in hundreds of stories and motion pictures. It has been called "one of the most spectacular caravan trails in human history." At the height of its use, sometimes four and even eight wagons rolled abreast along the Santa Fe Trail. The route was packed so hard that for years parts of it could not be plowed.

The history of the trail contains numerous fascinating incidents. In 1830, the Prince of Württemberg (Germany) came on a hunting and exploring trip. The famous explorer and frontiersman Jedediah Smith was scalped by Indians near Ulysses, after losing his way on the trail. Gabe Wade, an ox-team freighter, is said to have captured and broken in a buffalo to pull his wagon when one of his oxen died. Some freighters used buffalo hide to cover the oxen's feet for protection in rocky areas. Kit Carson, the famous guide and scout, reportedly shot his own mule near Pawnee Rock because he thought it was an Indian.

Fortunes could be made in a single trip over the trail. Goods worth $15,000 might bring close to $100,000 in furs and gold at Santa Fe. During the years between 1822 and 1843, goods valued at $3 million passed over the Santa Fe Trail.

Later, settlers and the California Forty Niners (gold seekers) by the thousands joined the traders on the Santa Fe Trail, on their way to the Pacific Coast. It is estimated that ninety thousand people hurried across Kansas during their journey to California's goldfields.

The tremendous Oregon Trail passed through northeast Kansas, where thousands of emigrants and their wagons and goods crossed the plains. Near Olathe, the Santa Fe and the Oregon trails split, and someone put up an early highway marker with two signs pointing in different directions. One part read "Road to Oregon"; the other declared in an equally matter-of-fact way "Road to Santa Fe," although the two destinations were separated by 1,200 miles (1,931 kilometers) of wilderness.

To protect the travelers on the Santa Fe Trail, Colonel Henry H. Leavenworth built a small cantonment on the Missouri River in 1827. Appropriately enough, the first real "settlers" in Kansas were the son and daughter-in-law of the famous frontiersman Daniel Boone. Daniel Morgan Boone was sent by the national government

"Wagons Ho!" One of the Bicentennial wagon trains pauses in Kansas at Castle Rock (left) and continues on its way (below).

to the Leavenworth area in 1827 to teach farming to the Kansas Indians. He brought his wife, making them the first non-mission settlers in the territory, and on August 22, 1828, old Daniel Boone had a grandson, Napoleon Boone. He was the first non-Indian boy known to have been born in what is now Kansas.

Colonel Leavenworth's stronghold soon was called Fort Leavenworth in his honor, and it became the first permanent settlement in Kansas. Soon steamers brought an increasing number of immigrants to the beginning of the cross-country trails at Leavenworth.

GROWING PAINS

As late as 1854, the non-Indian population of Kansas consisted of only eight hundred settlers and seven hundred soldiers. But in that year Congress passed the Kansas-Nebraska Act, establishing each as a separate territory. This opened Kansas to settlement. The United States had by this time become strongly divided over the question of slavery. The Kansas-Nebraska Act declared that the people of these regions would have the privilege and responsibility of deciding whether their territories would be free or slave. Neighboring Missouri, a slave state, felt that Kansas must certainly become a slave state. Thousands of Missourians lived near the border, and many of them hurried over to settle claims in Kansas.

This alarmed the opponents of slavery. Many settlers had also come in from northern states—Iowa, Ohio, Illinois, Pennsylvania, and others—encouraged by various antislavery societies in the East.

In the election of March 30, 1855, proslavery forces overwhelmingly elected the territorial legislature by bringing in several thousand illegal voters from Missouri. Kansas's territorial governor was expected to either certify the election or be driven from the territory. This legislature has come to be called the Bogus Legislature, because of its extralegal status.

The legislature adopted new laws for Kansas, based almost entirely on the laws of Missouri. However, the legislators added the death penalty for anyone who incited the slaves to seek freedom,

Kansas state capitol painting, Tragic Prelude, John Brown, *by John Steuart Curry, shows the antislavery leader after a raid that killed five proslavery people.*

and they decreed a prison sentence for anyone who spoke or wrote against slavery.

This drastic repression alarmed slavery opponents throughout the country. They increased their efforts to persuade antislavery settlers to go to Kansas; arms and even some cannon were shipped in to protect their followers in the territory. A Free State party was organized in Kansas. It refused to recognize the Bogus Legislature and set up its own government.

The stage was now set for one of the most tragic series of events in the history of the United States. Kansas was to undergo a "little Civil War" several years before the main Civil War split the country.

In May 1856, a group of so-called Border Ruffians from Missouri made an armed attack on Lawrence, the principal Free State settlement. Areas of the town were looted and burned. John Brown, the radical antislavery leader, struck back and led a raid that killed five proslavery people near Pottowatomie Creek. In the months that followed, men were called from their beds and shot, women and children were driven from their homes, towns were sacked and burned, and outrages were committed on both sides. Frederick Brown, son of John Brown, was killed by proslavery raiders in August 1856. Even London newspapers sent reporters to cover events in Bleeding Kansas.

Five governors and five acting governors held office in seven years. The territorial capital, an observer wrote, "was moved about like a chessman, and three state constitutions were written and rejected."

As time went by, the Free Staters became stronger. They obtained a majority after the first year or two, but the Border Ruffians and other powers from across the Missouri border helped to keep the slavery forces strong.

For a fourth time a convention met, on this occasion in July 1859, at Wyandotte, now part of Kansas City, to write a new constitution for Kansas. This was approved by the people in the fall of 1859 and submitted to Congress. Sixteen months passed before the Kansas constitution was approved by Congress and Kansas was admitted as a free state. However, this happened only after several of the slave states had seceded from the Union and the Civil War was soon to begin.

On January 29, 1861, President James Buchanan signed the bill making Kansas the thirty-fourth state of the nation, with Dr. Charles Robinson as first governor. James H. Lane and Samuel Pomeroy were the first United States senators. In spite of civil strife and bloodshed, the population of Kansas had seen an incredible, almost unbelievable growth in the six years between 1854 and 1860, from almost nothing to 107,206.

Yesterday and Today

KANSAS AND THE CIVIL WAR

On February 22, 1861, the president-elect of the United States was traveling to Washington to take his oath of office when he paused to take part in a ceremony at Philadelphia. At historic Independence Hall, Abraham Lincoln made a brief speech, and for the first time a thirty-four-star flag was brought out. A newspaper of the time reported: "The flag was rolled up in a man-of-war style, then adjusted, a signal fired, and, amid the most excited enthusiasm, the president-elect hoisted the national ensign. A stiff breeze caught the folded bunting and threw it out boldly to the winds. Cheer followed cheer, until hoarseness prevented continuance."

In this dramatic way, the star of Kansas officially joined the national flag. It is probable that, as Lincoln watched the Kansas star rising into the sky, he remembered the visits he had made there when he spoke against slavery at Atchison and Leavenworth. One of the editors of a local Atchison paper did not even mention the speech because he supported another candidate.

Before long, the Civil War engulfed the nation. During the first days of the war, Kansas men took part in an unusual action. There were rumors that the president might be kidnapped, so Senator James H. Lane recruited a company of Kansas volunteers, called the Frontier Guard, to protect the president. They camped on the velvet carpet of the East Room in the White House. When the immediate danger was over, the men were dismissed with thanks.

Kansas now moved from a "cold war" to a shooting war. During much of the war, many Kansas communities were in danger from raids by Confederate guerrilla forces. As early as September 12, 1861, Humboldt was sacked by the Confederates.

Some of the fiercest raids of the Civil War were conducted in Kansas by William Clarke Quantrill. Guerrilla attacks reached their peak when Quantrill raided Lawrence on August 21, 1863, burning two hundred buildings and killing 150 innocent civilians. This has been called "the most devastating single incident of the Civil War in Kansas." A Kansas newspaper of the time wrote: "The few who heroically ran out with their guns were quickly murdered, as were, in fact, all who showed themselves during the first half hour. . . . After they had spread over town they commenced to plunder. . . . During all this time citizens were being murdered everywhere. Germans and Negroes . . . were shot immediately. . . .

"There were many heroic deeds performed by the ladies. In many instances they placed themselves between their husbands and fathers and danger when the drunken fiends held cocked pistols at them." In another of Quantrill's raids, at Baxter Springs, October 6, 1863, he attacked the Union troops, and ninety-six were killed.

Other battles in Kansas were fought between troops and guerrillas of both sides. However, the Battle of Mine Creek, on October 25, 1864, was the most notable engagement fought in Kansas during the Civil War. More than twenty-five thousand men took part in this battle. The Union victory ended the threat of a Confederate invasion of Kansas.

Kansas has an unusual record in the Civil War; it could boast of the highest percentage of its eligible men serving in the Union army of any of the Northern states. From its small population at the time, 20,149 Kansas men went into service—an amazing total. Also, more Kansas men in the Union forces died than men of any other Union state, in proportion to population. Loyal Indian forces in Kansas fought several battles against the Confederates.

During the war, of course, civil life continued in the state. Topeka was chosen the permanent capital in November 1861, and in 1862, Kansas' first governor was impeached, along with the state auditor and secretary of state. They were charged with a swindle in state bonds. The governor was acquitted, but the other officers were found guilty.

FRONTIER COW TOWNS

Fans of Western movies and television programs probably are quite familiar with the frontier cow towns of Kansas.

30

The first such settlement was established in 1864, when James R. Mead set up a trading post near the village of the Wichita Indians, which was located near the mouth of the Little Arkansas River. In 1865, Mead sent his helper, part-Indian Jesse Chisholm, into the southwest with a wagon filled with goods for trade. He returned with a load of buffalo hides so heavy that he cut deep tracks into the prairie. The route he blazed became the famous Chisholm Trail.

When the Union Pacific Railroad reached Abilene, Texas ranchers saw a chance to drive their herds to market, and in 1867, about two thousand head of Texas longhorns were driven up the Chisholm Trail and on to Abilene. So Abilene became the first major "cow town," and no one knows how many millions of cattle plodded their hot and dusty way over the Chisholm Trail. Probably more than a million went to Abilene alone between 1867 and 1871.

As soon as the cowboys delivered their cattle to the railroad yards and received their pay, most of them wanted to celebrate. As many as several hundred itinerant cowboys might be in town at the height of a drive.

Abilene was quick to oblige them by creating saloons, gambling houses, and all kinds of entertainment. Gamblers and other characters moved in to try to take some of the easy money. There was little respect for law and order among many of the independent cowboys and the lawless characters who tried to fleece them of their funds.

Abilene had two famous police officers—Tom Smith and James Butler Hickok. Their reputation as lawmen spread quickly across the country, especially the fame of "Wild Bill" Hickok.

As the railroads moved on, new towns took turns at being the closest market for Texas cattle, and each automatically became the most important cow town, where the cattle were driven for rail shipment. After Abilene came Newton, then Ellsworth, Wichita, Dodge City, and finally Caldwell, where the Chisholm Trail crossed the Kansas border into Oklahoma.

Each of these towns claimed to be the wildest, the wickedest, and the rip-roaringest in all the West. However, the most famous name is probably that of Dodge City, the "beautiful, bibulous Babylon of the frontier." The town was established in July 1872 and named in

Re-created Front Street in Dodge City is a reminder of the days when it had the reputation of being the most notorious street in the West.

honor of General Grenville M. Dodge. The first Santa Fe Railroad train arrived at Dodge City in September 1872, and before long Dodge City claimed to be the Queen of the Cow Towns. More than four hundred thousand Texas longhorns were shipped through Dodge during its reign as Cowboy Capital of America.

The names of its lawmen still appear on millions of television screens—Bill Tilghman, Mysterious Dave Mather, Prairie Dog Dave Morrow, Bat Masterson, and Wyatt Earp.

While these names have become legendary, those men were all real people, with more human weaknesses than some Western writers like to admit. The story is told that Wyatt Earp once "amateurishly loaded all six chambers of his revolver and blasted a hole through his coat."

Although most of the lawmen were honest much of the time, some had their moments of weakness. Henry Brown, the respected marshal of Caldwell, kissed his bride good-by and road off with accomplices to rob the bank at Medicine Lodge. They killed the cashier and shot the bank president. However, retribution was swift. Brown was killed attempting to escape, "his body riddled with bullets," and his partners were hanged twenty-four hours after the attempted robbery.

LIFE ON THE PRAIRIE

The quick money and excitement of the cow towns soon gave way to the more normal life of increasing numbers of settlers, who were content to earn their living the hard way—from the land. Beginning in about 1870, there was a great rush for Kansas land. Many immigrant groups came to the state to find new homes. A Russian group arrived at Cedarvale in 1871, and six hundred German Mennonites, who came by way of Russia, reached Kansas in 1874. Altogether, about fifteen thousand Mennonites came to Kansas to make their homes. Large numbers of Swedish people found a haven in the area of Lindsborg.

Life on the Kansas plains was not easy. There was not even

Because there was not enough wood for fence posts in Kansas, some posts were cut from rock. Some may still be seen in northcentral Kansas (above).

enough wood for fence posts, and in some areas posts were cut from rock with great difficulty. Fences with rock posts may still be seen in northcentral Kansas today. In western Kansas, where there was no wood for fires, settlers gathered buffalo chips (manure) for fires.

Houses were made of sod or by digging into the sides of hills. In the writings of one pioneer mother, she calls her home a "dug-out." She goes on to say: "Ours is dug four feet down, and has a frame part about five feet high on top of the ground. It is 12 x 20 inside, with a whitewashed ceiling and a canvas partition.... It is hard work to come west and make a home.... This year everything was a failure in this county. Everybody left that could, but we have a few cattle and enough corn stalks to keep them alive till grass comes.... We are 47 miles from the railroad and the only way to get a living is to freight. It takes four days to go to the railroad and back with a load. My man has gone for a load now. While he is gone I take care of thirteen head of cattle, two pigs, one colt, and milk four cows, do my house work, make lace and crazy patch.... I sleep with a double-barrelled shot-gun loaded in the closet and a revolver handy."

Great prairie fires often swept through the tall grasses, burning everything in their path. Hordes of grasshoppers, such as those in the invasion of 1874-1875, ate everything green, including, as someone remarked, the window shades.

The *Kansas Historical Quarterly* tells about another pioneer Kansas woman who lived near Cottonwood Falls. Some Kansa Indians passed by as "she was making lye soap in a big iron kettle outside her house. Three of the Indians came near the kettle and motioned that they wanted to eat from it. She kept shaking her head no, but could

This painting by Henry Lewis, Settlers Flee a Prairie Fire, *pictures only one of the dangers settlers faced on the prairies.*

not make them understand her. They simply thought she was unwilling to share with them. Finally one Indian took the spoon from her and took a big bite. Tears came to his eyes but he never changed the expression on his face. He passed the spoon to the Indian next to him, who ate with tears in his eyes and he in turn passed it on to the third, who did likewise. After which they turned and rejoined their party.''

BIGGEST POWWOW IN HISTORY

Relations between the settlers and the Indians were not always this peaceful. While the Civil War was still raging, there was a general Indian war in Kansas in 1864. By 1867, it seemed that both sides might be ready for peace. The United States government asked five tribes—Comanche, Apache, Cheyenne, Kiowa, and Arapahoe—to meet on the Medicine River near present-day Medicine Lodge to make a peace treaty in October 1867.

Fifteen thousand Indians met the government peace commissioners, who were escorted by five hundred troops. This was said to be the largest meeting of Indians and non-Indians ever to take place in the United States, and one of the most colorful "powwows" ever held. Henry M. Stanley, one of the several newsmen there, made the long trip from New York City to Medicine Lodge to report on the council for his paper. Stanley later gained fame in his search across Africa for Dr. Livingstone.

Some progress was made at this council toward getting the Indians' permission to build railroads and establish settlements. But the troubles continued. In the same year as the council, a squad of Union Pacific track layers were killed. General George Custer was stationed in Kansas, and his troops had many encounters with the Indians before he left his Kansas station for his fatal battle with the forces of Chief Sitting Bull.

In 1878, a group of about 350 Cheyenne decided to return from their reservation, in what is now Oklahoma, to their former home in the Dakotas. The Cheyenne's raid through Kansas caused great

36

excitement and often panic. Thirty-eight settlers and two soldiers were killed. However, all was not tragedy. The Dodge City newspaper said: "Emerson Brown reported killed by Indians, turns up with his scalp. He tells us that the Indians chased him five miles."

This was the last raid carried out by Indians in Kansas, and one historian has described it as "among the major Indian actions in Plains history."

FROM THE HALLS OF CONGRESS TO THE SHORES OF AGUINALDO

During the late 1800s many interesting events took place in Kansas or involved notable Kansans. Kansas, in 1880, became the first state to pass a prohibition amendment against liquor.

In 1882, although people in the East could hardly believe it possible, the Bethania Choirs of Bethany College gave their first performance of Handel's *Messiah*.

The town of Argonia claimed worldwide attention in 1887 by electing the first woman mayor in the history of the United states— Susanna Salter. Some claim that Mrs. Salter was the first woman mayor in the history of the world.

When financial depression hit Kansas, beginning in 1887, hundreds of people left the state, and the population dropped. It seemed to many that a new political party was needed, and the party of the people—the Populist party—came into being in Kansas in the 1890s. The Populists entered into a fusion ticket with the Democrats in 1892 and elected Lorenzo D. Lewelling as governor. They claimed control of the legislature. The Republicans, however, also claimed control and ejected the Populists from the legislative hall. The Populist governor called out the state militia and held the Republicans under siege for some time in what has been called the Legislative War. Later the United States Supreme Court decided in favor of the Republicans.

Some of Kansas's most interesting public figures were Populists. Mary Elizabeth Lease toured the state tirelessly for the Populist cause. Her advice to farmers was to "raise less corn and more hell."

When Jerry Simpson was running for Congress, he complained that his opponent was so wealthy he could wear silk socks. At that, his opponent walked over and pulled up Simpson's trouser leg. "He wears no socks at all," he said. The sympathy of the voters may have helped to elect "Sockless" Jerry Simpson, as he was known from that time on.

In 1893, Kansas was host to thousands of eager people in one of the most unique episodes in American history. The Indian lands in northeastern Oklahoma, known as the Cherokee Outlet, were to be opened to settlement. On September 16, countless numbers of people were poised along the southern border of Kansas, ready for the signal. At least fifty thousand were at Arkansas City and another fifteen thousand at Caldwell. The wild rush to claim Oklahoma land has been reported in many colorful accounts.

The war with Spain in 1898 brought fame to a Kansas hero, Colonel Frederick Funston, who captured Aguinaldo, the leader of the insurrection in the Philippines. Four Kansas regiments were enlisted for service in the Spanish-American War.

A FRESH NEW CENTURY

One of the first notable events of the twentieth century in Kansas was the devastating flood of 1903. Women were given the vote in 1912.

In World War I, General Leonard A. Wood trained troops at Camp Funston, one of the largest army camps in the nation; 80,261 Kansans saw service during the war, once again more than the state's quota in proportion to population.

When grain was desperately needed for the war effort, vast acreages were plowed and wheat and other crops were planted. This proved to be invaluable in feeding the world's hungry during wartime, as well as being profitable. But later, as Kansas's worst drought continued to dry up the fields in the thirties, it became clear that not enough thought had been given to conserving the land.

Strong and relentless winds swept across miles of unprotected

Colonel Frederick Funston leads the Twentieth Kansas Volunteers through Caloocan, the Philippines, after the battle. *Painting by G. W. Peters.*

prairies, carrying with the gale uncounted tons of Kansas soil. The choking dust storms of the Dust Bowl became a national disaster. One man, who did not lose his sense of humor, said the dust storms were so thick that the prairie dogs dug their holes in the air.

A personal tragedy came to Kansas when the famous Notre Dame football coach Knute Rockne was killed in an airplane crash near Bazaar in 1931. But Kansas had a part in an aviation triumph the following year, when Amelia Earhart Putnam of Atchison became the first woman to fly solo across the Atlantic Ocean.

In 1936, Governor Alf M. Landon of Kansas was named the Republican candidate for president. However, his opponent, President Franklin D. Roosevelt, was at the height of his popularity, and Landon failed to carry even his home state.

When World War II engulfed America, the nation was able to turn to Kansas for vast numbers of aircraft, because of the state's large aircraft industry. The airplane plants of Wichita employed sixty thousand people during the war. Another wartime contribution was the state's production of walnut blanks for gunstocks. Kansas was the leading producer of this war necessity.

Many Kansans, some 215,000 men and women, saw service in World War II. One of these was the supreme commander of the Allied Forces in Europe—General of the Army Dwight D. Eisenhower. At the war's end in 1945, General Eisenhower was greeted with a three-mile (five-kilometer) parade and great excitement in his home town of Abilene. Probably few in Abilene at that time could have foreseen the brilliant future in store for their town's favorite son.

In 1949, Kansas became a pioneer in an important activity in the field of medicine. Kansas's famous Rural Health Plan was adopted, and the first rural clinic was put in operation at Mankato. In order to provide first-class medical facilities to attract a doctor to their town, the people of Mankato raised funds and built and completely equipped a center for the most modern practice of medicine. The Kansas Rural Health Plan seeks to do as much as possible to encourage doctors to practice in small towns and rural areas.

The great floods of 1951 caused the almost unbelievable damage

The Eisenhower boyhood home in Abilene

of $2.5 billion in Kansas. The "floods" of 1952 were a flood of grain and a flood of ballots. That was the "bin-buster" year for Kansas wheat, the largest in history, when 307,629,000 bushels overflowed all storage facilities. The flood of votes for Abilene's Dwight Eisenhower swept him into the White House in the election of 1952, for the first of two terms.

It seemed strange to many people that Kansas, where freedom triumphed after much bloodshed, should bring itself national attention because of its segregation of blacks in the capital city's elementary schools. The famous case in which the United States Supreme Court declared school segregation unconstitutional was the case of

Brown v. *the Board of Education of Topeka,* decided in 1954. By the time the decision was given, however, most school segregation had disappeared in Kansas.

The worst tornado ever to strike Kansas hit the small town of Udall in 1955, almost completely destroying it. More than sixty-five persons were killed in Udall alone by the storm. However, although Kansas is troubled by tornados, its people quickly point out that its reputation as a tornado state is greatly exaggerated. Several other states are more often plagued by twisters than Kansas.

In 1961, Kansas became "one of the protectors of the free world," according to the *Topeka Capital-Journal.* Thirty-nine Atlas and Titan missile-launching sites were scattered across Kansas, where once the army cavalry fought Indians.

Also in 1961, Kansas celebrated the centennial of its statehood.

During the 1970s, world food shortages brought much Kansas land back to cultivation, and the energy crisis renewed interest in the search for oil and natural gas.

As they look forward toward the twenty-first century, residents of Kansas are willing to agree with *National Geographic* magazine that "no chapter in our western annals is more sheerly spectacular than the conquest of Kansas."

Natural Treasures

"It is undeniable beyond any doubt that Kansas is a paradise," wrote some of the Swedish settlers in Kansas. It is obvious that these land-loving people referred to the land itself. Certainly the soil that produces such bountiful crops is the state's greatest single natural treasure.

In–and under–the soil are other treasures not even dreamed of by the greedy Spaniards who thought that only gold, silver, or jewels were worth looking for. How could they know that the land some day would yield a black gold and an invisible gas worth more than the yellow gold they knew?

One of the largest reserves of natural gas known in the world is centered at Hugoton. Petroleum, helium, coal, clay, stone, gypsum, zinc, and salt are all found in Kansas. It has been said that "Hutchinson perches atop the greatest salt deposits in the world."

Although Kansas is not usually considered a timber state, forest reserves of several billion board feet of standing saw timber are a part of the wealth of the state. This is more lumber than has been used in all the past history of Kansas.

Most of the forests are comparatively new. It is thought that eastern Kansas had fairly good stands of timber when the first settlers came, but most of the virgin timber was used, often recklessly. Riverside Park in Wichita has one of the few remaining stands of virgin timber in the state. Settlers started to plant trees almost as soon as they arrived, and before too long the "sunburnt boom towns" had acquired shaded, cool streets. Beginning in 1935, the Prairie States Forestry Project was responsible for planting 3,541 miles (about 5,700 kilometers) of windbreaks to keep the soil from blowing away in dust storms and to help hold moisture. In 1963, Kansas entered the Tree Farm program. In this program, farmers have at least a minimum number of trees and care for them with good forest practices.

Commercial trees in Kansas include walnut, elm, ash, oak, sycamore, maple, pecan, hickory, basswood, black cherry, and cedar. Eastern red cedar is the only cone-bearing tree native to Kansas.

During the early years of exploration and settlement in Kansas, the most obvious wealth of the land was the unbelievable amount of big game. Probably nowhere in the world have there ever been such enormous numbers of huge and valuable animals, especially buffalo.

Many early Kansans noted that the very land beneath them sometimes shook under the galloping feet of thousands of buffalo. There may have been as many as twenty-five million buffalo roaming the American plains at one time. These were hunted without mercy. One man, William Cody, who came to be known as "Buffalo Bill," killed

Buffalo Hunt, *by Currier and Ives. During the early years of exploration and settlement on the plains buffalo were hunted without mercy by Indian and non-Indian alike. By 1875 they were nearly extinct.*

Prairie dogs such as this one (left) are now in danger of becoming extinct.

4,280 buffalo in eighteen months near Hays, to provide food for railroad workers.

A good buffalo hunter sometimes could earn $100 a day. Just for sport and excitement, passengers fired at buffalo from train windows as they passed. Most of those that were killed were left to rot unused. The hides were greatly in demand for buffalo robes, and at almost every western railroad station, great piles of buffalo hides were stacked waiting for shipment. One of these stacks is said to have contained forty thousand buffalo hides.

By 1875, the buffalo had been almost exterminated. So many had been killed that large numbers of people did a good business just in collecting bones for use as fertilizer. The bones were so valuable that they were said to be recognized as legal tender in Dodge City.

Today, the rabbit has replaced the buffalo as the most important game animal in the state. Jackrabbits are a nuisance to the farmer, however; three jacks can eat as much as a sheep. During the 1930s farmers held great "roundups," driving jackrabbits into fence corrals. Sometimes as many as fifty thousand were taken at one time.

Mink, raccoon, skunk, badger, bobcat, coyote, opossum, fox, muskrat, and squirrel are all fairly common in much of Kansas. A few armadillo are found. Only a few prairie-dog settlements now remain in the state. These animals have been exterminated as a pest. The prairie dog is not a dog but a kind of ground squirrel, with a barking call like a dog. Before long, this popular creature may become extinct.

Quail, prairie chicken, owl, hawk, eagle, jay, dove, duck, and geese are among the Kansas birds. At the Frank Robl Game Refuge near Ellinwood, twenty-two thousand migratory birds have been banded. They have been reported as far away as Alaska and the South American continent.

Sometimes in spring or fall, large numbers of seagulls fly into Kansas from the Gulf of Mexico. They are welcomed by farmers because they eat millions of insects, worms, and other pests.

Conservation of wildlife is important in Kansas. In the central part of the state, Maxwell State Game Preserve protects one of the state's largest buffalo herds, and Cheyenne Bottoms is one of the nation's outstanding wildlife refuges.

Fishing in Kansas yields a wide variety of catch, including large-mouth bass, bluegill, green sunfish, black crappie, catfish, white bass, walleye, and freshwater drum. Some flathead catfish reach weights of between sixty and seventy pounds (about twenty-seven to thirty-two kilograms).

Kansas waters yield a wide variety of fish and fishing is a popular sport in the state.

People Use Their Treasures

NATION'S BREADBASKET

The story of how Kansas became the Breadbasket of the Nation is an interesting one. Every major Kansas cereal crop was "imported"; none was native to the state. Beginning under the direction of James Wilson, United States Secretary of Agriculture from 1897 to 1913, experts such as Myers and Fairchild searched around the world to locate plants and trees that would grow and be used in Kansas.

However, it was another kind of expert who helped develop the major crop of Kansas. When the Mennonite settlers came to the Newton area in Kansas from Russia, beginning in 1874, one of their most important possessions was the bushel or so of seed grain that each of them carried. This grain was a strange red color, and since it came originally from Turkey, it was called Turkey Red hard winter wheat.

The Mennonites had grown this wheat in Russia, where they had fled to escape persecution in their native Germany. When they came to America to find religious and economic freedom, they were sure their hard winter wheat would do well in Kansas because the state's climate and soil were similar to those of their former Russian home.

How well it would do, however, no one could possibly have predicted. From this hard Turkey Red and other wheat strains has been developed the second largest single agricultural crop in the world, second only to Iowa's corn. It has made Kansas the nation's leading producer of wheat, accounting for about a fifth of all the wheat grown in the country.

Today, Hutchinson is the largest primary hard wheat market in the country. What are said to be the world's largest grain elevators soar into the sky at Hutchinson and Kansas City. In fact, Kansas

Turkey Red, a hard winter wheat, has helped make Kansas the nation's leading producer of wheat.

The Famarco grain elevator in Hutchinson is the world's largest.

possesses the largest capacity for grain storage in the nation. Dodge City calls itself the Buckle of the Kansas Wheat Belt. Abilene likes to think that it is the Heart of the Kansas Wheat Belt.

Wheat is not the only crop in Kansas, although it is the most important. Sorghum and corn rank next in total production. The world's largest hay market is also at Kansas City. The largest market in the world for broomcorn is located at Wichita. Kansas also ranks first among the states in silage production.

Garden City is the center of a large irrigated farming district in which grain sorghums, sugar beets, alfalfa, onions, and honeydew melons, as well as wheat, are among the important crops. During the dry years, this region was called "a land of gaunt cattle and loco weed."

Instead of depending on cattle from Texas, Kansas now has its own large and lively livestock industry. The largest covered railroad stockyards in the world are at Marysville. Each year one of the largest general roundups in the United States takes place at Elkhart. In 1963, more than five million cattle roamed the range or crowded the feed lots of Kansas. Today's figures, though smaller, are still substantial.

Altogether, the gross income of Kansas farms amounts to nearly $4 billion each year.

This Barber County pasture is in excellent range condition.

INDUSTRY

During the last forty years, Kansas has undergone a great transformation. More than eighteen hundred new industries took up locations in the state during that period, giving Kansas a more equal balance of manufacturing and agriculture.

The industrial plants in Kansas produce almost every product, from airplanes to zinc. Kansas manufacturers now produce goods each year with a total value of nearly $3.5 billion.

Kansas's first manufacturing plant, a sawmill, was built in the Kansas City area in 1852 by an Indian with the appropriate name of Matthias Splitlog. In that same year, the first gristmill, using waterpower, was constructed. When the hard wheat came, the early millers found it difficult to grind. The Mennonites actually had brought with them from Russia their large threshing stones. Turned by oxen, these ground the hard wheat into grain. Before many years, wheat-laden wagons lined up for blocks in season at Wichita, waiting their turn at the mills. Today, Kansas ranks first in the country in flour production.

Another agricultural industry had an early start in Kansas. The first slaughterhouse was established at Wyandotte, now Kansas City, in 1860. Today, Kansas City is one of the few cities where the large packing companies operate complete plants. The plants that manufacture animal serums at Kansas City are the largest in the world.

Probably the most spectacular manufacturing business in Kansas is the aircraft industry. Wichita leads the world in production of personal airplanes, with factories of such giants of the industry as Beech, Cessna, Gates, Learjet, and Boeing. More private aircraft are built at Wichita than in all the rest of the United States combined.

Jake Moellendick led the way in airplane manufacturing by investing his oil earnings in the early development of a most successful plane called the *Laird Swallow.* Clyde Cessna and Glenn Martin were other pioneers. By the mid-1920s Wichita was known as the Air Capital of the World. Fifteen different manufacturers were turning out aircraft there. Only four survived the stock market crash of 1929.

Wichita leads the world in production of personal airplanes.
This Beechcraft is being assembled at the city's Beech plant.

As part of the aerospace industry, Boeing produced the first stage booster for the Saturn moon rocket.

Forest products rank ninth in Kansas manufacturing. Timber industries produce more than $100 million worth of goods every year in the state.

Some Kansas manufacturing surprises include the leading producer of pre-cooked dog food machinery, at Sabetha, and the world's largest factory for the manufacture of carbon black, near Garden City. Among its many other uses, carbon black is used for black coloring in the paint industry.

Many leading national manufacturers have branch plants in Kansas, including General Motors, Colgate-Palmolive, Goodyear, Owens-Corning, and Du Pont.

MINERAL PRODUCTION

Kansas was the first state west of the Mississippi River to have a commercially producing oil well. This was Old Norman #1 at Neodesha, drilled in 1892. Since that time, the state has grown to be one of the major oil producers, ranking either seventh or eighth among the states for a number of years.

A Kansas man may have been the first person in the country to find a useful purpose for natural gas. He fixed jets on his cook stove and connected them by pipe to a natural gas source. Hugoton is said to be the first municipality ever to have title to its own gas well within the city limits.

Today, gas from the Hugoton fields is piped to many distant areas. In 1948, Standard Oil Company built a revolutionary plant at Garden City for producing synthetic gasoline from natural gas.

When a gas well was drilled successfully near Dexter in 1903, the town was elated. It held an elaborate ceremony to light the gas. Everyone was greatly disappointed when the gas not only failed to light but kept blowing out the flame of the lighting torch. Not until some time later was it discovered that this was one of the few sources in the world for rare helium gas. Four Kansas helium plants now produce the precious gas, and the one at Liberal is the world's largest.

Probably the earliest industry in Kansas was the production of salt; both Indians and early settlers evaporated salt from the brine of Seapo's 4,000-acre (about 1,620-hectare) salt marsh, in northcentral Kansas. Hutchinson is at present one of the nation's leading salt mining and processing centers. Salt was first discovered there in 1887.

For many years strip coal mines have been operated in the Pittsburg area. The world's largest producing volcanic ash mine is at Meade, and quartzite quarries are found at Lincoln. Galena, the center of lead and zinc mining and smelting, contains one of the world's largest smelters.

Altogether, more than twenty different minerals are produced commercially in Kansas for an annual value of almost one billion dollars.

TRANSPORTATION

Modern transportation reached Kansas for the first time as early as 1819, when the steamboat *Western Engineer* chugged past on its way up the Missouri River. For a time it was thought that much of the state might be covered by steamboat. The *Emma Harmon* in 1855 was the first steamboat to reach Lawrence, and steamboats were tried on the Kansas River for seven years, but it finally became clear that the state's internal rivers were not suitable for commercial steamboats. Only the Missouri River continued to bring a great volume of passengers and trade.

The great overland routes—the Santa Fe, Oregon, and Chisholm trails—remained supreme in Kansas inland travel and transport for many years. Another great trail across Kansas was that used in 1859 by the Fifty Niners, gold-seekers hurrying to the newly discovered gold fields near Denver, Colorado. In the 1850s, mail stagecoaches left daily for the seventeen-day round trip to Denver.

The famous Butterfield Overland Despatch Express terminated for a time at Atchison, and the even larger Russell, Majors, and Waddell freighters headquartered at Leavenworth. These freighting firms operated with 7,500 teamsters, 6,600 wagons, and 60,000 head of oxen. They carried millions of tons of freight through Atchison in a multimillion dollar business.

The even more famous but less successful Pony Express was founded by William H. Russell of Leavenworth. The *Leavenworth Daily Times* reported: "By telegram—'Have determined to establish a Pony Express to Sacramento, California, commencing the 3rd of April [1860]—Time 10 days. Signed Wm. H. Russell.'

"That's a short and important dispatch and the time to travel between here and California is very short also. The first conclusion almost anyone would come to is that this is utterly impossible." But it was not impossible, and the Pony Express riders have become the heroes of numberless legends, even though the operation lasted only eighteen months.

The first railroad did not reach Kansas until 1860. The *Free Press* of Elwood describes the great event: "On Thursday, July 19th, the people of Kansas and Missouri turned out in great numbers to celebrate the completion of the first section of the Elwood and Marysville Railroad. The cars ran from Elwood to Wathena every half hour through the day, and were constantly crowded. The ride was delightful, and every man seemed to regard it as a personal honor to take a trip on the first railroad yet built in our flourishing territory."

A city bond issue at Atchison gave the first support to the Atchison, Topeka and Santa Fe Railroad. The first Santa Fe line rails were laid on solid walnut ties, then the most available wood. In 1868 the Santa Fe began building westward from Topeka, and the first rail service on the line was available in 1869. Its general offices were established at Topeka.

Today, one of the world's finest airports at Wichita and the second longest network of highways in the country provide additional travel opportunities for the people of Kansas and its visitors. The travel industry in Kansas takes in several hundred million dollars each year.

NEWSPAPERS

It has been said that the history of journalism in Kansas is unique in all the world. In their book *Kansas in Newspapers,* Miller, Langsdorf, and Richmond declare that "Kansas is perhaps the only place" where "a newspaper was started before there was any news to print." In the opinion of pioneer Kansas editor D.W. Wilder, "Kansas, in a sense, is the child of newspapers."

The first newspaper ever published in Kansas was the first ever

56

published entirely in an Indian language. The *Siwinowe Kesibwi (Shawnee Sun)* was established in 1835 by Jotham Meeker at the Shawnee Baptist Mission. A typical sentence read: "Skiti lalammowita Siwinwike wesekitowewa, chena manwelaniwawewea wehmimaniwa cawekitake."

The first regular weekly was the *Kansas Weekly Herald* of Leavenworth. Type for its first issue, September 15, 1854, was set under a tree. An interesting article on "Western Energy" and the character of the people of the region appeared in its first issue.

According to Rolla A. Clymer, "The early-day editors were both rugged and valiant. The times called for boldness and plain speech—and they responded in kind. . . . They were peculiarly gifted with the necessary elements to infuse the Kansas paper with the rare and distinctive flavor it has borne ever since."

Many newspapermen of worldwide prominence achieved their fame in Kansas journalism, and some of them, including William Allen White, are discussed in a later section.

One of Kansas's most unusual and controversial newspapers was the *Appeal to Reason*. This socialist paper had a circulation of more than 200,000. It boasted that special issues sometimes reached a circulation of 2,250,000. The spectacle of a huge printing plant working night and day to produce millions of copies of a newspaper in the small Kansas town of Girard was a strange one indeed.

E. Haldeman-Julius took over the *Appeal to Reason* in 1912. Later this publisher's famous Little Blue Books on a multitude of subjects sold in fantastic quantities—in the many millions of copies—one of the greatest productions in American publishing history.

Over the years, Kansas has a record of more newspapers per capita than any other state. In the period between 1854 and 1936, 4,386 newspapers had been published at one time or another in the state.

In another field of communication, the first regular weather reports ever given over the radio were broadcast from the state college at Manhattan in 1912.

PLACE
OF
MEDITATION

Human Treasures

FIVE STARS

At the close of World War II, a reporter asked Mrs. Ida Eisenhower to give her feelings about her famous son. With a very slight smile, she asked him which one he meant. To Mrs. Eisenhower, all five of her sons were "stars."

Few persons at that time would have had any difficulty in identifying Kansas's most famous son, a five-star general who commanded the greatest military force the world had ever known and later became the president of the United States of America—Dwight David Eisenhower.

Dwight Eisenhower was not born in Kansas, but his parents brought him to Abilene when he was only one year old. There he grew to maturity.

While most people know of his major accomplishments, many are not so familiar with his extensive education and long career of public service. In addition to his degree from West Point, Eisenhower graduated from the Infantry Tank School, Command and General Staff School, Army War College, and the Army Industrial College. He served in the War Department and in the office of the chief of staff. He spent four years in the Philippines on the staff of General Douglas MacArthur. Later, he was chief of the War Plans Division of the War Department General Staff. In 1943 he became commander in chief of Allied forces in North Africa. At the climax of his military career, Eisenhower directed the Allied attack against Germany as supreme commander of the Allied forces in Europe, with the five-star rank of general of the army.

After being commander of the occupation forces in Europe, he returned to the United States to become chief of staff. Eisenhower served as president of Columbia University from 1948 to 1950, but took a leave of absence from that post to assume responsibility as

Opposite: The Eisenhower Chapel in Abilene.

commander of the North Atlantic Treaty Organization (NATO) forces in Europe.

When he was only nineteen, the *Dickinson County News* reported a speech Dwight Eisenhower had made at Abilene, called "The Student in Politics." The paper quoted him: A young man "naturally concludes, that with the Republican party splitting up and a number of honest and fearless ones tending toward Democracy, that the Democrat Party deserves his first vote. And ... the first vote generally determines his political standing" from that time on. Forty-three years sometimes changes a man's thinking, and it was as a Republican that Dwight David Eisenhower took the oath of office as thirty-fourth president of the United States on January 20, 1953. His electoral vote for a second term in 1956 was even larger than it had been in his first defeat of Adlai Stevenson.

As Mother Eisenhower pointed out, all of her five sons won positions of respect in their communities, although the others were overshadowed by their most famous brother. Milton Eisenhower won wide recognition as president of Kansas State University at Manhattan. He later became president of Pennsylvania State College and Johns Hopkins University and was a leader in Republican policy making.

OTHER PUBLIC FIGURES

Another Kansas political figure with a unique background was Charles Curtis, born in 1860 near Topeka. His father was a Kansas pioneer, and his mother was an Indian princess. Curtis grew up among the Kaw Indians, raised by his mother's mother, during a time when his tribe still went to war with the Cheyenne.

Later, he was sent to his father's parents for schooling. Curtis was anxious to return to the Indian way of life, but his Indian grandmother would not permit it. Charles Curtis had many careers, including those of jockey and lawyer, United States congressman and senator, before becoming vice president of the United States under Herbert Hoover. This is the highest public office attained so far by anyone of Indian descent.

60

Alf M. Landon of Topeka served with distinction as governor of Kansas, although he probably is better known as the man who suffered the worst defeat of any major presidential candidate in the country's history.

A number of women have played colorful parts in Kansas political life. In 1949, President Truman appointed former actress Georgia Neese Clark of Richland treasurer of the United States. Her signature appeared on millions of pieces of paper money. Susanna Salter of Argonia, who was probably the world's first woman mayor, was nominated as a joke with little thought that she could win. The famous woman Populist campaigner Mary Elizabeth Lease also began her political career accidentally. She ran into a labor meeting to get out of the rain and was so interested she became, according to one historian, "one of the most eloquent critics of the old order."

John J. Ingalls was a "golden-tongued" orator of Kansas. As United States senator from Kansas during the late 1800s he attracted the popularity which was to give him a place as one of Kansas's representatives in the national Hall of Fame in the Capitol at Washington. Governor George Washington Glick occupies the other Kansas niche in the Hall of Fame.

Frank Carlson of Concordia, congressman from 1934 to 1946, governor of Kansas from 1947 to 1950, and United States senator beginning in 1950, is one of the most prominent Kansans of Swedish descent. Harry H. Woodring was another prominent former governor, who served as secretary of war under Franklin Roosevelt.

SEASONED WITH SAGE

William Allen White, the Sage of Emporia, was a man unique in American history. He never held political office; he had no position of power in industry and never had great wealth or social position. Yet it has been said, "few individuals in American history have dominated the affairs of their state and colored the course of national political events more than William Allen White. . ."

Few also have made their impression on human affairs by living

61

their life almost entirely in a small town in a Midwestern state. White worked as a reporter for a short time on Kansas City newspapers. Then he bought the *Emporia Gazette* in 1895 and settled down to make it the nation's best-known small-town newspaper.

An early editorial called "What's the Matter with Kansas" attracted the attention of the eastern politician Mark Hanna, who had hundreds of thousands of copies of it circulated throughout the country. This was the beginning of White's fame as a political writer.

When he was arrested in 1922 because he thought a state law was opposed to freedom, White wrote his renowned editorial on freedom. For this he was awarded a Pulitzer Prize. One of the best-known tributes ever written, and the writing for which White probably will be most remembered, was his tribute in 1921 to his young daughter Mary just after her accidental death. *Mary White,* a television movie based on this tribute, was highly acclaimed.

William Allen White was also the author of a number of popular books, including *The Court of Boyville, Stratagems and Spoils,* and *Masks in a Pageant.*

When William Allen White died in 1944, the *El Dorado Times* wrote about the funeral: "They came—the captains and the kings . . . or they sent messages of regret and respect as did the President and others eminent in many fields. . . . He was the outstanding editor of his day. There is none to compare with him in the annals of Kansas—and few in the nation. He gave the country press a luster which it had not hitherto attained; there was not an editorial chair in the country which he could not have graced."

A posthumous Pulitzer Prize was awarded in 1947 for *The Autobiography of William Allen White.*

His son, William L. White, who died in 1973, also gained fame as an author and journalist.

SKIES ARE NOT CLOUDY ALL DAY: ART, MUSIC, LITERATURE

Probably very few persons know the musical team of Kelley and Higley, yet these men made a notable contribution to American music. Dr. Brewster Higley wrote a poem about his dugout home on the banks of Beaver Creek in Smith County, and the poem was first printed in the *Smith County Pioneer* in 1873. Later, the poem was put to music by Daniel Kelley. Gradually it came to be known to more and more people and was given the title "Home on the Range." The song was reported to be a favorite of Franklin D. Roosevelt, as it is of many others. It will undoubtedly continue as one of the most enduring of our national melodies, as well as the state song of Kansas.

Another Kansas theme, the Indian, was used in the music of composer Thurlow Lieurance, a professor at the University of Wichita. His best-known work was "By the Waters of Minnetonka."

A Kansas author wrote "the best-selling novel of all time." The Reverend Charles M. Sheldon was minister for many years of Central Congregational Church of Topeka. When he wanted a new approach to his Sunday evening sermons, he gave a series of talks about a modern man who tried to live his life as Christ might have done in the modern world. Out of these sermons came his best-selling book *In His Steps.* Over the years this book has sold close to thirty million copies in more than thirty-five languages.

Another Kansas author who gained distinction was Edgar Watson Howe. His *Story of a Country Town* was named by William Allen White "one of the ten best novels written in America." Howe was known as the Sage of Potato Hill. White also said of him, "E.W. Howe is the most remarkable man Kansas or the Middle West has produced."

Dr. Arthur E. Hertzler built a hospital at Halstead and practiced in the community. His autobiography, *Horse and Buggy Doctor,* helped make him a nationally known figure.

Native Kansans were also part of the twentieth-century literary scene. William Inge, playwright and author of such works as *Come Back, Little Sheba, Picnic,* and *Bus Stop,* was born in Independence. The short-story writer Damon Runyon was a native of Manhattan. Edgar Lee Masters, the author of *Spoon River Anthology,* was born in Garnett.

Kansas artists include John Steuart Curry, born in Jefferson

County in 1897. His controversial mural *Tragic Prelude* is one of the highlights of the Capitol Building at Topeka. The well-known Swedish teacher and artist Birger Sandzen taught for many years at Bethany College in Lindsborg.

HERO IN THE PHILIPPINES

In 1901, there were few Americans who did not know of Frederick Funston, of Allen County. As a young man, Funston had a number of adventures. He studied the flora of Alaska and spent the winter alone on the forbidding banks of the Klondike; he paddled 1,500 miles (2,414 kilometers) down the Yukon River to the Bering Sea. When he learned of the plight of Cuban patriots, he hurried to enlist in the Cuban army.

When the United States went to war with Spain in 1898, Funston was appointed colonel of the Twentieth Kansas Infantry, which eventually was sent to the Philippines. When his father asked him what he knew about military tactics, his son answered, "Not much, but I am halfway through this book on the subject, and by the time I reach San Francisco, I will have mastered it."

For heroism under fire in the Philippines, Funston received the Congressional Medal of Honor. America did not recognize the independence of the Philippines, and guerrilla warfare continued under the direction of Philippine insurrectionist commander Emilio Aguinaldo. General Funston conceived a plan to capture Aguinaldo by posing with a group of insurrectionists. The plan moved forward smoothly and swiftly, and Aguinaldo was captured almost before his forces realized what was taking place.

The capture electrified the American people, and General Frederick Funston became a national hero. In 1906, he was in charge of military forces in the San Francisco area when the earthquake struck. His handling of the situation there added greatly to his reputation. If his death of a heart attack had not occurred in 1917, just before the United States entered World War I, it is thought he might have been offered the leadership of American forces in Europe, which later was given to General John Pershing. General Funston was only fifty-one at the time of his death.

SUCH INTERESTING PEOPLE

Another unique Kansan was Carry Nation, of Medicine Lodge. Although Kansas legally became a prohibition state in 1880, there were still many saloons. Carry Nation gained national fame by smashing these in a very spectacular way, beginning in her home county. She was arrested twenty-five times for her actions in taking hatchets to saloons all over the country. This, however, only gained more prominence for her crusade. After her death in 1911, her followers put up a monument to Carry Nation at Union Station in Wichita. It is a strange fact that the monument was later knocked over by a beer truck and never replaced.

Lydia B. Conley, a Kansan of Indian descent, was the first woman ever permitted to plead a case before the United States Supreme Court. She appealed the decision of Congress to take away the Wyandot burial ground at Kansas City.

Two other Kansas women, Amelia Earhart Putnam and Osa Johnson, gained fame for bravery in their adventurous careers. Amelia Earhart Putnam, born in Atchison in 1898, is probably the world's most famous woman aviator. Her flights across the Atlantic, and later the Pacific, where she disappeared without a trace, are still considered epic adventures.

Osa Johnson and her husband, Martin, both grew up in southeast Kansas. They wrote, made films, and lectured about their adventures in Africa and gained a worldwide reputation as jungle experts. After Martin's death in a California plane crash, Osa Johnson carried on their work alone.

In the field of health, Kansas has produced a number of leading figures and one quasimedical man of particularly colorful reputation—John R. Brinkley.

Many experts would call Topeka the "mental health center of the world" because of the work of Menninger Clinic. Topeka is probably the only place where there are more psychiatrists than doctors in all other fields. The clinic was begun by Dr. Charles Frederick Menninger and carried on by his sons, Doctors Will and Karl.

A Dodge City doctor, Samuel J. Crumbine, became a leading campaigner for better public sanitation. Crumbine pointed out the health hazards of the common drinking cup and the unsanitary public roller towel. He also crusaded against the dangers of the common house fly. Crumbine gained international recognition for his methods of fighting tuberculosis and typhoid.

Dr. John R. Brinkley established his practice at Milford, Kansas, in 1917. Before long, he established one of the early radio stations in the state and, using his station, began to advertise that he had perfected a method of restoring youth by transplanting goat glands. Soon he had founded a modern hospital, and people were coming to him from all over the world.

However, some other doctors began to call him a quack, and his license to practice medicine was revoked.

When he found his practice ruined, Dr. Brinkley, in 1930, decided to run for governor of Kansas an an independent. His name was not on the ballot, so he ran as a write-in candidate. He conducted a breathtaking campaign, using his radio station to great advantage. It is often said that if his write-in ballots in that first election had all been counted, Brinkley would have won. He still received 183,278 votes, only 33,893 behind the winner.

In the field of sports, the man called by many the greatest pitcher in the history of baseball, Walter Johnson, was born in Humboldt and made his home at Coffeyville. He pitched in the major leagues for twenty-one years and won 416 games, ranking him second. He also holds major league records for the most career strikeouts, 3,508, most career shutouts, 113, and lowest career earned-run average, 2.37. The Pottawatomie Giant, heavyweight boxer Jess Willard, took his nickname from his home county in Kansas. He was six feet six inches (two meters) tall and weighed 250 pounds (113 kilograms). He won the world's heavyweight championship from Jack Johnson in a twenty-six round fight in Cuba in 1915. He held the title for four years until defeated by Jack Dempsey.

66

Teaching and Learning

The first free school in Kansas was established by the Wyandot Indians in 1844. Many of the Eastern Indian tribes that came west brought a considerable degree of civilization with them, "more than many pioneer whites," according to some authorities.

White children also went to school in Kansas at the Shawnee Manual Labor School, starting in 1848, and at Council Grove in 1854. Before the end of the century, Kansas adopted a statewide system of city high schools. The plan for these was proposed by Professor J.H. Canfield of the University of Kansas, father of noted novelist Dorothy Canfield Fisher.

Only four years after settlement became legal in Kansas, two institutions of higher education were founded—Baker University at Baldwin and Highland College. St. Benedict's College was founded at Atchison in 1859, only a year after Baker and Highland. St. Benedict's is known for its "million dollar monastery." Baker University began at Baldwin in the Old Castle building, which is still on the campus and is the oldest college building in the state. The Bishop Quayle Collection of Bibles at Baker University is one of the finest collections of rare Bibles. Two copies of the original King James version of the Bible and Bibles handprinted by monks are among the prizes in the collection.

Classes began at the University of Kansas in Lawrence in 1866. One of the features of the campus is the Snow Entomological Museum. It includes more than two million insect specimens and is considered one of the most complete in the United States. The Medical Center of the University of Kansas is located at Kansas City.

Another state-supported university is Kansas State University at Manhattan. It was established in 1858 as Bluemont College, a Methodist institution, and came under state control in 1863. It gained national attention when Milton Eisenhower, brother of the president, was president of the university.

One of the best-known small colleges in the Midwest is Bethany College at Lindsborg. Bethany had its beginnings as a Swedish Lutheran institution.

The Bethany College Campus at Lindsborg, with the Wallerstedt Library in the background.

Another prominent church-related college is Bethel College in North Newton, the oldest and largest Mennonite college in America.

The University of Wichita, said to be the first municipal university established west of the Mississippi, became Wichita State University in 1964. It was long known as Fairmount College, a Congregational school. Also at Wichita is Friends University.

Ottawa University at Ottawa came into being through the generosity of the Ottawa Indians, who contributed 20,000 acres (8,094 hectares) of land for the establishment of this Baptist school. Haskell Indian Junior College at Lawrence is the largest Indian school in the United States. Other higher education institutions include Washburn University, Topeka; Emporia Kansas State College, Emporia; Kansas State College of Pittsburg; Fort Hays Kansas State College, Hays; and the College of Emporia.

Altogether, the young men and women of Kansas may select from twenty-seven four-year colleges and universities within their state.

Enchantment of Kansas

THE NORTHEAST

Kansas's first incorporated city, Leavenworth (June 1854), has sometimes been called the Mother-in-Law of the Army because so many army officers have married Leavenworth women. For many years it was the largest city in Kansas. The city serves two dissimilar institutions—the great federal penitentiary and Fort Leavenworth.

Fort Leavenworth is the oldest military post in continuous operation west of the Missouri River. The United States Army's Command and General Staff College is located there, and it maintains an interesting museum.

The founder of Fort Leavenworth, General Henry Leavenworth, is buried in the national cemetery. Another military man, General Ulysses S. Grant, is honored here with a statue by the famous sculptor Lorado Taft.

Atchison is an interesting Missouri River town. It was in Atchison, in 1859, where Abraham Lincoln first tried out ideas for the speech he delivered later at the Cooper Union in New York. The Cooper Union speech is often said to have helped Lincoln gain the presidency of the United States.

A memorial plaque at Memorial Hall in Atchison reminds visitors that one of the world's great railroads, the Atchison, Topeka and Santa Fe, was organized there. The railroad actually was organized by a $500,000 bond issue put out by the city.

On a bluff overlooking the Missouri, at Atchison, Amelia Earhart Putnam, one of the world's greatest women aviators, was born. In a different kind of claim to fame, the city is also the location of the largest cold-storage facility of its kind. This was created from a former limestone mine of 16.5 acres (6.7 hectares).

Within a year after they had reached the junction of the Kansas and Missouri rivers, the Wyandot Indians had built a school, church, store, and council house. This settlement was the beginning of Kansas's second largest city. Later, seven other towns in the area, including Wyandotte, merged to form Kansas City, Kansas.

Aerial view of Kansas City

When Wyandot Indians, some now living in Oklahoma, petitioned Congress for permission to sell the Wyandot burial grounds in a very valuable area of Kansas City, one of the Wyandot descendants, Lydia B. Conley, padlocked the cemetery gates and put up a shelter she called Fort Conley, where she mounted guard. Mainly because of her efforts, the cemetery has been preserved as part of Huron Park.

There is considerable rivalry between the two separate parts of the Kansas City metropolitan area, that of Missouri and of Kansas. The people of Kansas like to point out that a large share of the manufacturing plants of the area are located on the Kansas side.

The city of today is a major milling, livestock, grain storage, meat-packing, and transportation center. The Central Baptist Theological Seminary and State School for the Blind are also located there.

The State School for the Deaf operates at nearby Olathe. The city has taken the nickname of the Cowboy Boot Capital because of its nationally known boot manufacturers.

The first band and first community church in Kansas were formed at Lawrence in 1854. Since the founding of the first church, according to Emory Lindquist, "Kansas churches, Protestant and Catholic alike, have rendered distinguished service to the state through a wide variety of institutions. Academies, colleges, hospitals, homes for the aged, children's homes, and other agencies devoted to the ministry of mercy have brought great blessings across the years. The churches have a continuous record of constructive service to humanitarian causes in various relief and aid programs."

Although Lawrence, as the headquarters for antislavery forces, was burned and sacked twice before it was ten years old, it fought back vigorously. A monument in Oak Hill Cemetery stands in memory of the 150 victims of Quantrill's raid. Another memorial is the lofty campanile on the University of Kansas campus, dedicated to the dead of World War II. Another university landmark is its famous lilac hedge, a tremendous line of purple bloom.

Lawrence's neighboring city, Topeka, the capital, is one of the most unusual cities of its size in the country. Even its name is unusual—taken from the Indian, it means "a good place to dig edible roots" (potatoes).

Topeka was founded in 1854 through the efforts of Cyrus K. Holliday, a young man who had come from the East with $20,000 and a strong desire to build a great railroad. He and several other pioneers chose the site of what is now Topeka to build a railroad center. The company that was formed, with Holliday as president, succeeded not only in founding the city, but in building the Atchison, Topeka and Santa Fe Railroad as well.

The railroad company presented to the state a twenty-acre (eight-hectare) tract for a capitol building, which was begun in 1866. Its design is similar to the Capitol in Washington. The building was not finished in its present form until 1903. The green dome rises to a lofty 304 feet (93 meters).

The murals of the capitol are world renowned. Those on the second floor are by a noted muralist, John Steuart Curry. Newer murals on the first floor are by a Topeka artist, David H. Overmyer.

Another local artist, sculptor Robert Merrel Gage, created the well-known statues of Abraham Lincoln and the *Pioneer Woman* on the capitol grounds.

The Kansas State Historical Society and Museum are especially outstanding. The society's newspaper files are the largest in America except for the Library of Congress—a fitting tribute to Kansas's unique place in the history of journalism. Another prize of the museum collection is a Spanish sword of the time of Coronado (1541), found on the plains of Kansas.

Still another unique historical memento is the flagpole on the grounds of Topeka High School. This was taken from the mast of the historic naval ship *Constitution (Old Ironsides)*.

Topeka's Menninger Foundation has given the city its reputation as the Rochester of psychiatric care and treatment, a reference to the home town of the famous Mayo Clinic.

The Capper (now Stauffer) Publications have their headquarters in Topeka. The old home of Charles Curtis is also located here.

Topeka is the home of large railroad repair shops of the Atchison, Topeka and Santa Fe.

Another historic Kansas structure, moved from its original location, is the old Dutch windmill in the park at Wamego. This landmark was brought stone-by-stone from its original farm site twelve miles (nineteen kilometers) away.

Nearby Manhattan is home of Kansas State University. The museum and parks of Manhattan are unusual for a community of its size. Near Manhattan is the recreational area created by the building of Tuttle Creek Dam and Lake.

Fort Riley, just west of Manhattan, is one of the largest of all inland military reservations. The first capitol building of Kansas has been restored and may be seen at Fort Riley, which covers the site of the old town of Pawnee, the original territorial capital.

The state capitol building in Topeka (above) has a distinctive green dome. The territorial capitol building at Fort Riley (left), the state's first capitol, has been restored. Below: The grounds and buildings of Topeka's Menninger Foundation.

SOUTHEAST

Council Grove has often been called "the most historic site on the Santa Fe Trail." Here the Indians gathered for their powwows before settlement by Europeans. Coronado may have camped in the area during his search for the riches of Quivira. The historic treaty with the Indians opening the Santa Fe Trail was also signed here.

Under Post Office Oak at Council Grove, travelers placed their letters to be picked up and carried back by other travelers going the opposite way. At the Last Chance store, travelers had the final opportunity to buy supplies, since there was no other supply station to the west until the trail's end at Santa Fe. Council Grove was chosen as the location for the Madonna of the Trail monument, a tribute to the heroic women who made so many sacrifices on the long hard journeys.

To the south, at Cottonwood Falls, another monument marks the site of the airplane accident where the famous Notre Dame football coach Knute Rockne lost his life.

At Emporia, the memory of one of Kansas's best-known men, William Allen White, is kept alive everywhere. Peter Pan Park was donated to Emporia by the Whites in memory of their daughter Mary. The park contains the well-known bust of Mr. White by prominent sculptor Jo Davidson.

Lyndon has some small measure of fame because of its Runt Park, with a statue dedicated to a dog named Runt.

Ottawa, where the Reverend Jotham Meeker taught the Indians, is the location of his grave. Famous speakers and artists often came to Ottawa as part of its Chautauqua program. These included William Jennings Bryan, Rutherford B. Hayes, William McKinley, and Clarence Darrow.

Near Ottawa, the town of Silkville once stood. Silkworms and experts in silk were brought here from France by Ernest Boissiere. Unfortunately, the silk industry did not succeed in this locality.

Garnett, south of Ottawa, was the birthplace of Senator Arthur Capper, who also was the first native Kansan to be elected governor.

Few towns the size of Osawatomie are so well remembered

throughout the country. This community has become known as the home area of John Brown, the fiery opponent of slavery. People feel very strongly about Brown. Some consider him a hero; others, a traitor and a fool. A cabin that he used and a statue of the abolitionist leader stand in John Brown Memorial Park there.

Buildings still remain of old Fort Scott, established in 1842, and the national cemetery near Fort Scott is said to be the first to be established in the nation. At Chanute, where Osa Leighty Johnson was born, the Safari Museum contains trophies collected by Mrs. Johnson and her famous husband, Martin. The Johnsons are buried at Chanute. Humboldt is known for its annual parade of floats featuring scenes from the Bible. By contrast, Baxter Springs once called itself "the toughest town on earth."

Coffeyville is probably best remembered for an event that took place in 1892. On October 5, the notorious Dalton gang brazenly carried out its plans to rob two Coffeyville banks at the same time.

The alarm was given, and local hardware stores threw open their supplies of arms to citizens, who ducked behind wagons and other handy shelters and began shooting into the banks. By one account, "Rheumatic old men who had hobbled with difficulty a moment before, dived into convenient barrels with acrobatic agility." The bandits ran out of the banks into heavy crossfire. Four citizens and four of the Dalton gang were killed in an area that became known as Death Valley.

As the local newspaper reported next day, "The trains over the four principal roads leading to the city have brought hundreds of visitors to the scene of the bloody conflict." This has been called "certainly the most famous street fight in the history of the old West."

Another Dalton, Emmett, age sixteen, survived, although he had been shot twenty-three times. After serving a term in prison, he was released and turned to real estate and contracting in southern California, where he died at sixty-six, it was said, "chastened and reformed."

Coffeyville has a museum dedicated to these citizen-defenders against the Daltons. The museum also features a Walter Johnson

Wichita, in central Kansas (above), is the state's largest city.

Memorial, honoring the baseball hero, and souvenirs of Wendell Willkie, who taught there.

CENTRAL KANSAS

Wichita, in central Kansas, is the state's largest city. Modern metropolitan Wichita is a strange contrast to the prairie village of grass lodges built there by the Wichita Indians in the early 1860s. The famous cow town developed here in 1872. Then, as someone wrote, "Where cattle had built dance halls and gambling houses, wheat built churches and schools."

Modern Wichita preserves an unusual part of its past. Historic Wichita, Inc., has reconstructed the community as it looked in its cattle days. It is called Cowtown Wichita. The first log house, hotel, jail, and church have all been moved to the cow town. A blacksmith shop, printing house, general store, land office, feed mill, millinery shop, railroad station, and post office typical of the period can be seen there.

The National Flying Farmers organization has its headquarters at Wichita, and the National Semi-Pro Baseball Tournament offers an exciting "little world series" there each year. In the field of music, the Wichita Symphony is rapidly gaining renown.

To the south, more than 200,000 tulips bloom in springtime at Belle Plaine.

At Wellington, the local museum has one of the most unusual collections—two thousand canes of all types. Actor Fred Stone lived at Wellington during part of his youth.

Every five years a great pageant is held at Medicine Lodge to commemorate the 1867 treaty with the Indians. More than fifteen hundred people take part in the pageant, which is one of the most elaborate of its kind in the country. The road between Medicine Lodge and Coldwater is noted for its forty-two mile stretch (about sixty-eight kilometers) of beautiful cedar trees, called Cedar Tree Lane.

The story of old Runnymede, near Harper, has been called "one of the most fantastic in all of Kansas's curious history." The town was founded by Ned Turnly in 1887, and settled by upper-class English people, who brought their Tally-ho coaches, butlers, and other accompaniments and wore top hats, white ties, and similar clothes that seemed strange on the Kansas prairie. Only one tombstone is left at the site of the town to tell the tale of this short-lived trial at elegant country living.

In the early days of Hutchinson, the area was surrounded by a plowed furrow to guard against prairie fires. Its streets were marked off with buffalo bones. The "builder" of Hutchinson's first house was A.F. Horner, who won a lot as a prize. It was later discovered that he had won similar prizes in four other towns by moving his house from place to place. Today, Hutchinson is the Salt Capital of the World.

Newton is a center of the Mennonite settlements of Kansas. The first worldwide meeting of the Mennonite church on the North American continent was held at Newton in 1948. Most Mennonites consider Bethel College at Newton to be the group's greatest cultural achievement. The college houses documents that are said to prove that the Mennonites first brought Turkey Red hard winter wheat to Kansas. Another helpful device brought by the Mennonites was a grass burner, a stove that could use the prairie grass for fuel, a great blessing in barren areas.

Nearby Hillsboro is headquarters for the Mennonite Brethren of North America.

Among other valued trophies at the museum of McPherson College in McPherson is the world's first man-made diamond.

Nearby Lindsborg, the center of Kansas's Swedish community, is widely known for the outstanding quality of its music and art. The noted performance of Handel's *Messiah* has been given on both Palm Sunday and Easter since 1889. Since 1892, artists of international reputation have often been engaged for the solo parts, and the chorus now numbers five hundred trained voices. Some of the non-professional musicians have sung in every performance for more than fifty years. Concerts and recitals continue all through Holy Week and attract music lovers from distant places.

In another field of art, painter Sven Birger Sandzen gained world fame at Lindsborg. The Sandzen Museum is a high point of a visit to the community.

Bethany College at Lindsborg was founded by Dr. Swensson. The college's school of art uses a building of remarkable history—the Swedish pavilion of the St. Louis World's Fair of 1904. This was moved to Bethany as a gift of the Swedish government.

Probably nowhere else in America is the art of woodcarving so generally practiced. The quality of the carving is usually very high, and the community is one of the best-known in America for its wood masterpieces, many of which are on display in local stores.

Although many Swedish customs have been maintained, the days

Svensk Hyllnings Fest is a Swedish festival held every other year in Lindsborg, the center of the state's Swedish community.

of old live only in descriptions such as the one written by a local editor about Christmas 1881. He was called from his bed by the church bell at four in the morning. Christmas morning was "clear, starlit and pleasant. The city was already illuminated, nearly every house had tapers in the windows and the farm houses out on the prairie, as far as the eye could see." Every window of the church gleamed with candles. The choir sang a Swedish Christmas anthem.

Times were not equally good to everyone in the Swedish community. Another account tells of Swedish people taking up a collection for a neighbor who had died. They managed to get only six dollars for lumber for a coffin.

In 1903, a flood inundated four-fifths of Salina, but the city was quickly restored. The importance of wheat in this area is emphasized by the fact that the Roman Catholic church there is designed to resemble a grain elevator. West of Salina, the Brookville Hotel is the oldest operating hotel in Kansas. To the south at Coronado Heights, Coronado is supposed to have set up his camp, and pieces of chain mail of the type used by Spaniards have been found in the area.

79

Large stone markers in memory of Father Juan Padilla, the priest who accompanied Coronado, have been erected at Herington and near Lyons.

The Eisenhower Memorial Museum, library, and boyhood home at Abilene are popular tourist attractions. The buildings are located on land once plowed and planted by the five Eisenhower brothers. The museum contains souvenirs and mementos of the military and political career of Dwight D. Eisenhower. In the city library at Abilene is the doll collection of Mrs. Mamie Eisenhower.

On the Abilene post office lawn a boulder marks the end of the extended Chisholm Trail. Old Abilene Town of frontier days has been re-created, and it is said that tracks made by buffalo in the old days may still be seen in some places near Abilene. The National Coursing Meet at Abilene is called the "world series" of greyhound racing.

The round formations of Rock City, near Minneapolis, are said to be unique in the world. Delphos has national fame as the old home of Mrs. Grace Bedell Billings. As a young girl, Grace Bedell wrote the famous letter to Abraham Lincoln suggesting that he grow a beard. This he did and acknowledged the little girl's suggestion with thanks.

The half-mile (.8-kilometer) banked dirt auto racing track at Belleville is said to be the fastest of its kind in the world.

WHERE THE WEST IS TAMED

Nationwide attention was once given to the little town of Lebanon when it was the geographical center of the United States. Since Alaska and Hawaii have become states, the geographical center of the country has moved to Oregon, but Lebanon is still the nearest town to the geographical center of the forty-eight contiguous states.

Near Smith Center is the log cabin home of Dr. Brewster Higley, author of the poem about the Kansas prairie that became famous as the song "Home on the Range."

Travelers on the plains are able to see the spires of a great church for many miles before reaching the town of Victoria. Its twin towers soar 140 feet (about 43 meters) into the sky. This is St. Fidelis Church, known as the Cathedral of the Plains, which was erected by German-Russian immigrants. To build it, each parishioner was assessed forty-five dollars and six loads of stone.

Before the German settlers, Victoria was occupied by wealthy Englishmen, who rode after jackrabbits and coyotes in regulation red hunting outfits. They even dammed Big Creek to have enough water for a steamboat which they brought overland by oxcart. Although the English introduced the successful Aberdeen Angus cattle to the United States, the colony failed and was taken over by the German

St. Fidelis Church, the Cathedral of the Plains, in Victoria.

immigrants. These newcomers had left their adopted homes in Russia because their religious freedom had been taken away. Much of the town during this period was built to resemble a Russian village.

Famed auto magnate Walter Chrysler's boyhood home was at Ellis. For those interested in sod houses, one of the best re-created examples today is at Colby. It is headquarters for the organization called Sons and Daughters of the Soddie. All who have lived in or even attended church in a sod house may become members. Several other sod houses may be seen in other parts of the state.

A marker near Beeler locates the old Carver homestead, from which George Washington Carver, the world-famous black scientist, went out to greatness. The old stone blockhouse of Fort Hays is now a museum at Hays, where a Kansas state college is located.

The metropolis of western Kansas is Garden City. Its Windsor Hotel, with a three-story lobby, was called the Waldorf of the Prairies, and many celebrities stayed there. It is now closed. The Oakarah Herb Gardens is one of the unusual attractions of the area.

Liberal is known as the "key city" of the Hugoton-Oklahoma-Texas Panhandle area. However, a stranger claim to fame is its International Pancake Race. On Shrove Tuesday, housewives in both Liberal and Olney, England, run a quarter of a mile (four-tenths of a kilometer) with a pancake in a skillet, tossing it twice on the way.

The International Pancake Race is held every year in Liberal.

Old Fort Larned (above) is a National Historic Site.

The Coldwater area was noted for its Comanche Cattle Pool in the early 1880s. This was 84,000 acres (34,000 hectares) of pasture which at one time was enclosed by a single continuous fence.

Few towns of Greensburg's size can boast two outstanding tourist attractions. The first is reportedly the world's largest hand-dug well, 109 feet (33 meters) deep and 32 feet (10 meters) in diameter. Visitors can walk down long flights of steps to the water level. The second major attraction of Greensburg is the largest Pallasite meteorite ever found, which is displayed along with many other items in the Celestial Museum.

Old Fort Larned near Larned has been made a National Historic Site. The fort was named in honor of Colonel Benjamin F. Larned, paymaster of the United States Army. It is likely no one was more popular with the troops than the army paymaster. It was the most important fort on the Kansas section of the Santa Fe Trail.

DODGE CITY, THE WILD WEST

The very name Dodge City means Wild West to people all over the world. In the early 1870s, it is said, two cowboys had a gun fight on a high point overlooking Dodge City. When one was killed, he was buried exactly where he fell. No one even bothered to take his boots off. This became notorious Boot Hill, where those who met a violent death in town during the early years were buried, sometimes with their boots on, sometimes wrapped in their blankets with their boots used for pillows. A dance hall girl, Alice Chambers, is said to have been the last person buried on Boot Hill.

Visitors today who expect to see Boot Hill as it was in the old days will be disappointed. The bodies were moved from the original Boot Hill to another cemetery to make way for a school. Today, the city hall stands where Boot Hill once was. Near the entrance is the Cowboy Statue, Dodge City's tribute to its early visitors who sometimes were almost as wild as the thousands of cattle they herded. The statue was created by Dr. O.H. Simpson, a city dentist.

Dr. Simpson was responsible for a hoax that fools many visitors even today. To give atmosphere to a Rotarian convention, Dr. Simpson created an imitation Boot Hill graveyard, with grave markers carrying names created by the dentist, such as Toothless Nell, One-Eyed Jake, and Shoot-'em-Dead Harry. The local Rotary planted a cottonwood tree to be the historical gallows tree. A rope noose dangling from a branch helps to create the proper effect in this mock cemetery, now a memorial to those who died in the early days.

The modern visitor can stroll down the re-created Front Street of Dodge City, much as it was in 1870s and 1880s when it gained the reputation as the "most notorious street in the West." In contradiction to the old days, only soft drinks are served in the wicked Long Branch Saloon. Old stores and other buildings on the re-created Front Street help to give the old-time effect. Here also is the famous

Opposite: An old stagecoach on reconstructed Front Street in Dodge City

museum collection started by Chalk Beeson, a prairie-scout police officer and prominent cowboy band leader. The museum contains relics of many prominent and notorious Dodge City people.

Of course, even in the days of the Wild West, most Dodge City residents went calmly about their business during the daytime and took no part in the night life. Others, such as the Reverend Luther Hart Pratt, attempted to reform the wicked. He gained his nickname, Fiddlin' Preacher, by going into the saloons, playing a catchy tune on his violin to capture attention, then preaching a short sermon and asking everyone to come to church services on Sunday. Often someone would pass a ten-gallon hat in the saloon and take up a collection for the fearless minister.

In an effort to maintain its reputation, Dodge City in 1884 staged one of the few bullfights ever held in the United States. Outside officials informed the sponsors of the fight that such an affair could not be held in the United States. They promptly wired back claiming that Dodge City was not in the United States and went ahead with the program.

The *Dodge City Democrat* reported: "Promptly at 3 o'clock Capt. A.K. Moore of Paso del Norte, Mexico, manager of the fight, ordered the sounding of a trumpet and immediately the five bullfighters entered the arena ... in bullfighers' costume. At another sound of the bugle a door was opened and a wild and fierce looking Texas bull rushed into the ring....

"It was truly a grand and at the same time sorrowful sight to witness—grand to see the noble beast standing firm and defiant in the center of the ring, head erect and tail lashing the air, and sorrowful to think that human beings could torture a poor dumb brute in order to cater to the ... curiosity of the populace."

It is clear from this account that even in "wicked" Dodge City there was much of the sympathy and humanity that has since become so characteristic of all Kansas.

Handy Reference Section

Instant Facts

Became 34th state January 29, 1861
Capital—Topeka, founded 1854
Nickname—The Sunflower State
Motto—*Ad Astra per Aspera* ("To the Stars through Difficulties")
State animal—American buffalo
State bird—Western meadowlark
State tree—Cottonwood
State flower—Native sunflower
State song—"Home on the Range"
Area—82,264 square miles (213,063 square kilometers)
Rank in area—14th
Greatest length (north to south)—208 miles (335 kilometers)
Greatest width (east to west)—411 miles (661 kilometers)
Geographic Center—Barton (15 miles [24 kilometers] northeast of Great Bend)
Highest point—4,039 feet (1,231 meters), western border, north of U.S.
　　　　　highway 40
Lowest point—680 feet (207 meters), Oklahoma border, south of Coffeyville
Population—2,364,236 (1980 census)
Population rank—32nd
Center of population—In Chase County, 9 miles (14 kilometers) northwest of
　　　　　Cottonwood Falls
Population density—29 per square mile (11 per square kilometer), 1980 census
Physicians per 100,000—126

Principal cities—

Wichita	279,835	(1980 census)
Kansas City	161,148	
Topeka	115,266	
Overland Park	81,784	
Lawrence	52,738	
Salina	41,843	
Hutchinson	40,284	

You Have a Date with History

1541—Coronado searches for treasure
1719—Claude du Tisne crosses Kansas
1804—Lewis and Clark touch Kansas
1806—Zebulon Pike crosses Kansas
1824—First Christian mission in Kansas
1825—Indian treaties open Santa Fe Trail

1827—Fort Leavenworth established
1828—Napoleon Boone, first white boy born in Kansas
1854—Kansas-Nebraska Act establishes Kansas Territory
1861—Statehood; Topeka selected as capital
1863—Quantrill burns Lawrence
1865—Chisholm Trail is blazed
1867—Indian peace treaty of Medicine Lodge
1871—First Mennonites arrive in Kansas
1878—Last Indian raid in Kansas
1892—Populists elect governor
1912—Women gain full suffrage in Kansas
1917—World War I begins (80,261 Kansans in service)
1931—Knute Rockne dies in air crash near Bazaar
1936—Governor Alf Landon nominated for president
1941—World War II begins (215,000 Kansans in service)
1949—Rural Health Plan adopted
1951—Floods cause $2.5 billion damage
1952—Greatest wheat crop
1954— *Brown v. Board of Education of Topeka*
1975—Out-migration slowed
1976—Oil and gas exploration spurred by energy crisis
1986—Kansas, top producer of wheat and beef cattle, suffers as many banks close
and many farms are foreclosed

Thinkers, Doers, Fighters

People of renown who have been associated with Kansas

Al-le-ga-wa-hu
Carlson, Frank
Clark, Georgia Neese
  (later Mrs. Andrew J. Gray)
Cody, William Frederick
  (Buffalo Bill)
Curry, John Steuart
Curtis, Charles
Eisenhower, Dwight David
Eisenhower, Milton
Funston, Frederick
Haldeman-Julius, E.
Hertzler, Arthur E.
Hickok, James Butler (Wild Bill)
Higley, Brewster
Howe, Edgar Watson
Ingalls, John J.
Inge, William

Johnson, Martin
Johnson, Osa
Johnson, Walter
Kelley, Daniel
Landon, Alfred M. (Alf)
Lieurance, Thurlow
Menninger, Charles Frederick
Menninger, Karl
Menninger, Will
Nation, Carry
Putnam, Amelia Earhart
Russell, William H.
Sandzen, Sven Birger
Sheldon, Charles M.
Swensson, Carl
White, William Allen
White, William L.
Willard, Jess.

Sunflowers, the state flower, may be seen all over Kansas in summer.

Governors of the state of Kansas

Charles Robinson 1861-1863
Thomas Carney 1863-1865
Samuel J. Crawford 1865-1868
Nehemiah Green 1868-1869
James M. Harvey 1869-1873
Thomas A. Osborne 1873-1877
George T. Anthony 1877-1879
John Pierce St. John 1879-1883
George W. Glick 1883-1885
John Alexander Martin 1885-1889
Lyman Underwood Humphrey 1889-1893
Lorenzo D. Lewelling 1893-1895
Edmund Needham Morrill 1895-1897
John W. Weedy 1897-1899
William Eugene Stanley 1899-1903
Willis Joshua Bailey 1903-1905
Edward Wallis Hoch 1905-1909
Walter Roscoe Stubbs 1909-1913
George Hartshorn Hodges 1913-1915
Arthur Capper 1915-1919

Henry J. Allen 1919-1923
Jonathan M. Davis 1923-1925
Ben S. Paulen 1925-1929
Clyde M. Reed 1929-1931
Harry H. Woodring 1931-1933
Alf M. Landon 1933-1937
Walter A. Huxman 1937-1939
Payne Ratner 1939-1943
Andrew F. Schoeppel 1943-1947
Frank Carlson 1947-1950
Frank L. Hagaman 1950-1951
Edward F. Arn 1951-1955
Fred Hall 1955-1957
John McCuish 1957
George Docking 1957-1961
John Anderson, Jr. 1961-1965
William H. Avery 1965-1967
Robert Docking 1967-1975
Robert Bennett 1975-1979
John Carlin 1979-

*Keeper of
the Plains,
Wichita.*

Index

page numbers in bold type indicate illustrations

Abilene, 31, 40, 41, 49, 58, 59, 80
Agriculture, 15, 49-51
Aguinaldo, Emilio, 38, 64
Aircraft industry, 40, 52, **53**
Airplanes, 40, 52
Airports, 56
Al-le-ga-wa-hu (Chief), 20
Allen County, 64
Animal, state, 87
Animals, 44, 45
Apache Indians, 36
Appeal to Reason, 57
Arapahoe Indians, 36
Archeology, 17
Area of state, 87
Argonia, 37, 61
Arkansas City, 38
Arkansas River, 12
Artists, 63, 64, 72
Atchison, 29, 55, 56, 65, 67, 69, 71
Atchison County, 21
Atchison, Topeka and Santa Fe Railroad, 56, 69, 72
Authors, 63
Auto racing, 80
Baker University 67
Baldwin, 67
Barber County pasture, **51**
Baseball, 66, 76, 77
Basins, 12
Baxter Springs, 30, 75
Bazaar, 40
Becknell, W.H., 23
Beech aircraft plant, **53**
Beeler, 82
Beeson, Chalk, 86
Belle Plaine, 77
Belleville, 80
Bethania Choirs, 37
Bethany church, Lindsborg, 9, 10
Bethany College, **8,** 37, 64, 67, **68,** 78
Bethel College, 68, 78
Bibles, Bishop Quayle Collection, 67
Bicentennial wagon trains, **25**
Big Basin, 12
Big Creek, 81
Billings, Grace Bedell, 80
Bird, state, 87
Birds, 46
Blacks, 30, 41
"Bleeding Kansas," 28
Blind, State School for, 71

Bluegrass festival, Winfield, **95**
Bluemont College, 67
Blue River, 12
Bluestem Belt, 11, **11**
Bogus Legislature, 26, 27
Boissiere, Ernest, 74
Boone, Daniel, 24
Boone, Daniel Morgan, 24
Boone, Napoleon, 26
Boot Hill, 85
Border Ruffians, 27, 28
Boxing, 66
Breadbasket of the Nation, 49
Brinkley, John R., 65, 66
Brookville Hotel, 79
Broomcorn, 50
Brown, Emerson, 37
Brown, Frederick, 28
Brown, Henry, 33
Brown, John, 27, **27,** 28, 75
Brown County, 15
Brown v. Board of Education of Topeka, 42
Buchanan, James, 28
Buffalo, 18, 19, 23, 44, **44,** 45, 46
Buffalo Hunt (painting), **44**
Bullfight, Dodge City, 86
Butterfield Overland Despatch Express, 55
Caldwell, 31, 33, 38
California gold rush, 24
Camp Funston, 38
Canes, museum collection, 77
Canfield, J.H., 67
Capital, state, 30, 71
Capital, territorial, 28, 72
Capitols, state, 27, 64, 71, 72, **73**
Capper, Arthur, 74
Capper Publications, 72
Carl Gustaf XVI, King of Sweden, 8
Carlson, Frank, 61
Carson, Kit, 24
Carver, George Washington, 82
Castle Rock, **25**
Catlin, George, 20
Cattle, 31, 50, 51, 81
Cedar Bluff Dam, 12
Cedar Tree Lane, 77
Cedarvale, 33
Celestial Museum, 83
Central Baptist Theological Seminary, 71
Central Congregational Church, Topeka, 63

Central Plains, region, 11
Cessna, Clyde, 52
Chalk Pyramids, 12
Chanute, 75
Chautauqua programs, 74
Cherokee Outlet, 38
Cheyenne Bottoms, 46
Cheyenne Indians, 19, 36, 60
Chisholm, Jesse, 31
Chisholm Trail, 31, 55, 80
Chronology, 87, 88
Churches, 9, 10, **58,** 63, 71, 79, 81, **81**
Chrysler, Walter, 82
Cimarron River, 12, 23
Cities, principal, 87
Civil War, 29, 30
Clark, Georgia Neese, 61
Clark, William, 21
Clark County, 12
Climate, 14
Clymer, Rolla A., 57
Coal, 43, 54
Cody, William "Buffalo Bill," 44
Coffeyville, 66, 75
Colby, 82
Coldwater, 77, 83
Colleges, 67, 68
College of Emporia, 68
Colonel Frederick Funston leads the Twentieth Kansas Volunteers (painting), **39**
Comanche Cattle Pool, 83
Comanche Indians, 36
Command and General Staff College, U.S. Army, 69
Communication, 56, 57
Concordia, 61
Congress, U.S., 21, 26, 28, 38, 60, 65, 70
Congressional Medal of Honor, 64
Conley, Lydia B., 65, 70
Conservation, 46
Constitution (Old Ironsides), 72
Constitution, state, 28
Corn, 50
Coronado, Francisco Vasquez, **16,** 17, 18, 72, 74, 79
Coronado Heights, 79
Cottonwood Falls, 35, 74
Council Grove, 67, 74
Council Grove, Pawnee Indian Council (painting), **22**
Cowboy Boot Capital, 71
Cowboys, 31
Cowboy Statue, Dodge City, 85

Cow towns, 31, 33, 76
Cowtown Wichita, 77
Crops, 49, 50
Crumbine, Samuel J., 66
Currier and Ives, 44
Curry, John Steuart, **27**, 63, 72
Curtis, Charles, 19, 60, 72
Custer, George, 36
Dalton, Emmett, 75
Daltons (outlaws), 75
Dams, 12, 72
Davidson, Jo, 74
Deaf, State School for, 71
Delphos, 80
Democratic party, 37, 60
Dempsey, Jack, 66
Density of population, 87
Depression, financial, 37
Dexter, 54
Dickinson County News, 60
Dodge, Grenville M., 33
Dodge City, 17, 31, **32,** 33, 37,
    45, 50, 66, **84,** 85, 86
Dodge City Democrat, 86
Drought, 38
Dust Bowl, 40
Dutch windmill, Wamego, 72
Du Tisne, Calude, 18
Earhart, Amelia, 40, 65, 69
Earp, Wyatt, 33
Education, 67, 68
Eisenhower, Dwight David,
    40, 41, 59, 60, 80
Eisenhower, Dwight David,
    boyhood home, **41**
Eisenhower, Ida, 59
Eisenhower, Mamie, 80
Eisenhower, Milton, 60, 67
Eisenhower Chapel, Abilene,
    58
Eisenhower Memorial
    Museum, 80
El Dorado Times, 62
Elkhart, 51
Ellinwood, 46
Ellis, 82
Ellsworth, 31
El Quartelejo, 20
Elwood and Marysville
    Railroad, 56
Elwood Free Press, 56
Emma Harmon (steamboat),
    55
Emporia, 62, 68, 74
Emporia Gazette, 62
Emporia Kansas State College,
    68
Ethnic groups, 33
Exploration, 17, 18, 21
Fairmount College, 68
Famarco grain elevator, **50**
Farming, 15, 49-51
Fence posts, rock, 34, **34**

"Fiddlin' Preacher," 86
Fifty Niners, 55
Fires, prairie, **20,** 35, **35**
Fish and fishing, 46, **47**
Fisher, Dorothy Canfield, 67
Flags, U.S., 22, 29
Flint Hills region, 11, **11**
Floods, 40, 41, 79
Flour production, 52
Flower, state, 87, **89**
Forests, 43, 53
Fort Hays, 82
Fort Hays Kansas State
    College, 68, 82
Fort Larned, 83, **83**
Fort Leavenworth, 26, 69
Fort Riley, 72, 73
Fort Scott, 75
Forty Niners, 24
Fossils, 15
Frank Robl Game Refuge, 46
Free State party, 27, 28
French in Kansas, 18
Friends University, 68
Frontier Guard, 29
Front Street, Dodge City, **32,**
    84, 85
Funston, Frederick, 38, **39,** 64
Gage, Robert Merrel, 72
Galena, 54
Garden City, 50, 53, 54, 82
Garnett, 74
Geodetic center, U.S., 11
Geographic center, state, 87
Geographic center, U.S., 80
Geography, 11
Geology, 12, 15
Girard, 57
Glacier, 15
Glick, George Washington, 61
Governors, state, 28, 30, 37,
    40, 61, 74, 90
Governors, territorial, 26, 28
Grain elevators, 49, **50**
Grant, Ulysses S., 69
Grasshopper plagues, 35
Great Plains region, 15
Greensburg, 83
Greyhound racing, 80
Guerrilla raids, Civil War, 29,
    30
Gunstocks, 40
Gypsum Hills, 12
Haldeman-Julius, E., 57
"Hallelujah Chorus," 9
Hall of Fame, 61
Halstead, 63
Handel, George Frederick, 9,
    37, 78
Hanna, Mark, 62
Harper, 77
Haskell Indian Junior College,
    68

Hay, 50
Hays (city), 45, 68, 82
Helium, 43, 54
Herington, 80
Hertzler, Arthur E., 63
Hickok, James Butler ("Wild
    Bill"), 31
Highest point, state, 87
Highland College, 67
High Plains region, 11
Highways, 56
Higley, Brewster, 62, 63, 80
Hillsboro, 78
Historic Wichita, Inc., 77
Holliday, Cyrus K., 71
"Home on the Range," 63, 80
Hoover, Herbert, 60
Horner, A.F., 77
Horse and Buggy Doctor, 63
Horses, 18
Howe, Edgar Watson, 63
Hugoton, 43, 54, 82
Humboldt, 29, 66, 75
Huron Park, Kansas City, 70
Hutchinson, 43, 49, 50, 54, 77
Ice Age, 15
Immigrants, 33
Independence (town), 63
Indians, 17, 18, 19, **19,** 20, 21,
    22, 23, 24, 26, 30, 31, 35,
    36, 37, 57, 60, 65, 67, 68,
    69, 70, 74, 77
Industry, 52, 53
Ingalls, John J., 61
Inge, William, 63
International Pancake Race,
    82, **82**
Irving, Washington, 15
Jackrabbits, 45
Jefferson, Thomas, 21
Jefferson County, 63-64
Jesuit missions, 23
John Brown Memorial Park,
    75
Johnson, Jack, 66
Johnson, Martin, 65, 75
Johnson, Osa, 65, 75
Johnson, Walter, 66, 75
Johnson County, 23
Journalism, 56, 57, 61, 62, 72
Junction City, 17
Kanopolis Dam, 12
Kansa Indians, 18, 20, 35
Kansas, derivation of name,
    18
Kansas City, 21, 28, 49, 50,
    52, 62, 65, 67, 69, 70, **70,** 71
Kansas Historical Quarterly, 35
Kansas in Newspapers, 56
Kansas-Nebraska Act, 26
Kansas River, 12, 21, 55, 69
Kansas State Historical Society
    and Museum, 72

92

Kansas State College, 68
Kansas State University, 60, 67, 72
Kansas Territory, 26, 27
Kansas Weekly Herald, 57
Kaw Indians, 18, 60
Keeper of the Plains, Wichita, **90**
Kelley, Daniel, 62, 63
Kickapoo, 23
Kiowa Indians, 36
Laird Swallow (airplane), 52
Lakes, 12
Lake Wilson, **14**
Landon, Alf M., 40, 61
Lane, James H., 28, 29
Larned, Benjamin F., 83
Larned, 83
Last Chance store, Council Grove, 74
Lawmen, 31, 33
Lawrence, 27, 29, 55, 67, 68, 71
Lead, 55
Lease, Mary Elizabeth, 37, 61
Leavenworth, Henry H., 24, 26, 69
Leavenworth, 24, 26, 29, 55, 57, 69
Leavenworth Daily Times, 55
Lebanon, 80
Legislative War, 37
Legislature, state, 37
Legislature, territorial, 26
Length, greatest, state, 87
Lewelling, Lorenzo D., 37
Lewis, Henry, 35
Lewis, Meriwether, 21
Liberal (city), 54, 82
Lieurance, Thurlow, 63
Lincoln, Abraham, 29, 69, 72, 80
Lincoln (city), 54
Lindquist, Emory, 71
Lindsborg, 8, 9, 10, 33, 64, 67, 68, 78, 79
Little Arkansas River, 31
Little Blue Books, 57
"Little Civil War," 27
Livestock, 50, 51
Long Branch Saloon, Dodge City, 85
Louisiana Territory, 21
Lowest point, state, 87
Lyndon, 74
Lyons, 80
Madonna of the Trail monument, 74
Manhattan, 12, 57, 60, 63, 67, 72
Mankato, 40
Manufacturing, 52, 53
Marais des Cygnes River, 12

Martin, Glenn, 52
Marysville, 51, 56
Masters, Edgar Lee, 63
Masterson, Bat, 33
Mather, Mysterious Dave, 33
Maxwell State Game Preserve, 46
McGovern, George, 61
McPherson, 78
McPherson College, 78
Mead, James R., 31
Meade, 54
Meat packing, 52
Medical Center, University of Kansas, 67
Medicine Lodge, 12, 19, 33, 36, 65, 77
Medicine River, 36
Meeker, Jotham, 23, 57, 74
Memorial Hall, Atchison, 69
Menninger, Charles Frederick, Will, and Karl, 66
Menninger Clinic, 65
Menninger Foundation, 72, **73**
Mennonite Brethren of North America, 78
Mennonites, 33, 49, 52, 78
Messiah of Handel, 8-10, 37, 78
Meteorite, 83
Milford, 66
Mine Creek, Battle of, 30
Minerals and mining, 43, 54, 55
Minneapolis, KS, 12, 80
Missile-launching sites, 42
Missionaries, 23
Missouri, 26, 27, 70
Missouri River, 21, 24, 55, 69
Moellendick, Jake, 52
Monument Rocks, **13**
Morrow, Prairie Dog Dave, 33
Motto, state, 87
Museums, 67, 69, 72, 75, 77, 78, 80, 82, 83, 86
Mushroom Rocks, **13**
Music, 8-10, 37, 62, 63, 77, 78
Musical America (magazine), 10
Nation, Carry, 65
National cemetery, 69, 75
National Coursing Meet, 80
National Flying Farmers, 77
National Geographic magazine, 42
National historic site, 83, **83**
National Semi-Pro Baseball Tournament, 77
Natural gas, 42, 43, 54
Nemaha County, 15
Neodesha, 54
Neosho County, 23

Neosho River, 12
Newspapers, 56, 57, 62, 72
Newton, 31, 49, 78
Nickname, state, 87
Nodaway River, 21
North Atlantic Treaty Organization, 60
North Newton, 68
Oakarah Herb Gardens, 82
Oak Hill Cemetery, Lawrence, 71
Oakley, 12
Oil, 42, 54
Oklahoma, 31, 36, 38, 82
Olathe, 24, 71
Old Abilene Town, 80
Old Norman #1 oil well, 54
Olney, England, 82
Olsson, Olof, 10
Oregon Trail, 24, 55
Osage Indians, 18, 23
Osawatomie, 74
Osborn, Joseph, 10
Osborne, 11
Ottawa, 68, 74
Ottawa Indians, 23, 68
Ottawa University, 68
Overmyer, David H., 72
Padilla, Juan de, 18, 80
Pancake Race, 82, **82**
Panhandle area, 82
Parks, 43, 70, 72, 74, 75
Pawnee (town), 72
Pawnee Indians, 18, 19, 21, **22**
Pawnee Rock, 24
Penitentiary, Leavenworth, 69
People, 88
Pershing, John G., 65
Peter Pan Park, Emporia, 74
Peters, G.W., 39
Petroleum, 42, 43, 54
Picurie Indians, 19
Pike, Zebulon, 21, **22**
Pioneer Woman (statue), 72
Pittsburg, 54, 68
Pixley, Benton, 23
Pomeroy, Samuel, 28
Pony Express, 55
Population figures, 26, 28, 87
Populist party, 37, 61
Post Office Oak, Council Grove, 74
Pottawatomie Creek, 28
Potwin, 12
Prairie dogs, 45, **45**
Prairie Fire (painting), **20**
Prairie fires, **20**, 35, **35**
Prairie States Forestry Project, 43
Pratt, Luther Hart, 86
Prehistoric times, 14, 15, 17
Presidents, U.S., 21, 28, 29, 40, 41, 59, 60, 61

Prohibition, liquor, 37, 65
Pulitzer Prizes, 62
Putnam, Amelia Earhart, 40, 65, 69
Pyramids (rock formations), 12
Quantrill, William Clarke, 29, 30, 71
Quartzite, 54
Quivira, 17, 74
Radio weather reports, 57
Railroads, 31, 36, 56, 59
Rainfall, 14
Remington, Frederic, 16
Republican party, 37, 40, 60
Republican River, 12
Republic County, 22
Richland, 61
Rivers, 12
Riverside Park, Wichita, 43
Robinson, Charles, 28
Rock City, 12, 80
Rockets, 53
Rock fence posts, 34, **34**
Rockne, Knute, 40, 74
Roosevelt, Franklin D., 40, 63
Runnymede, 77
Runt Park, Lyndon, 74
Runyon, Damon, 63
Rural Health Plan, 40
Russell, Majors and Wadell, freighters, 55
Russell, William H., 55
Sabetha, 53
Safari Museum, Chanute, 75
St. Benedict's College, 67
St. Fidelis Church, 81, **81**
Salina, 17, 79
Saline River, 12
Salt, 43, 54, 78
Salter, Susanna, 37, 61
Sandzen, Sven Birger, 64, 78
Sandzen Museum, 78
Santa Fe, NM, 23, 24
Santa Fe Railroad, 33, 56, 69, 71, 72
Santa Fe Trail, 23, 24, 55, 74, 83
Schools, 41, 67
Scott City, 12
Scott County, 20
Seagulls, 46
Seapo, 54
Segregation, 41
Senators, U.S., 28, 29, 60, 61, 74
Settlers Flee a Prairie Fire (painting), **35**
Seymour, Samuel, 22
Shaw, 23
Shawnee Baptist Mission, 57
Shawnee Manual Labor School, 67

Shawnee Methodist Mission, 23
Shawnee Sun, 57
Sheldon, Charles M., 63
Silkville, 74
Simpson, "Sockless" Jerry, 38
Simpson, O.H., 85
Sitting Bull (Chief), 36
Siwinowe Kesibwi, 57
Slavery, 26, 27, 28
Smith, Jedediah, 24
Smith Center, 80
Smith County, 63
Smith County Pioneer, 63
Smoky Hill River, 12
Snow Entomological Museum, 67
Sod houses, 34, 82
Soil, 15, 18, 43
Solomon River, 12
Song, state, 63, 87
Sons and Daughters of the Soddie, 82
Sorghum, 50
Spanish-American War, 38, **39, 64**
Spanish in Kansas, 17-19, 22
Sphinx (chalk rock formation), 12
Spoon River Anthology, 63
Stagecoaches, 55
Stanley, Henry M., 36
Statehood, 28, 42
Statistics, 87
Stauffer Publications, 72
Steamboats, 55, 81
Stevenson, Adlai, 60
Stone, Fred, 77
Story of a Country Town, 63
Sunflowers, **89**
Supreme Court, U.S., 37, 41, 65
Svensk Hyllnings Fest (Swedish festival), **79**
Swedish people, 8, 33, 78, 79
Swensson, Alma, 9, 10
Swensson, Anna, 10
Swensson, Carl, 9, 78
Symbols, state, 87
Taft, Lorado, 69
Texas, 82
Tilgham, Bill, 33
Timber, 43, 53
Topeka, 30, 56, 60, 61, 63, 64, 65, 68, 71, 72, 73
Topeka Capital-Journal, 42
Topeka High School, 72
Tornadoes, 42
Tragic Prelude, John Brown (painting), **27,** 64
Transportation, 55, 56
Tree, state, 87
Tree Farm program, 43

Trees, 43, 77
Truman, Harry S., 61
Turkey Red hard winter wheat, 49, 78
Turnly, Ned, 77
Tuttle Creek Dam, 12, 72
Twentieth Kansas Infantry, **39,** 64
Udall, 42
Ulysses, 24
Union Pacific Railroad, 31, 36
Universities, 67, 68
University of Kansas, 67, 71
University of Wichita, 63, 68
Verdigris River, 12
Vice President, U.S., 19, 60
Victoria, 81
Volcanic ash, 54
Wachtmeister, Wilhem, 8
Wade, Gabe, 24
Wagon trains, 23, 24, **25**
Walnut River, 19
Wamego, 72
Washburn University, 68
Wathena, 56
Well, hand-dug, world's largest, 83
Wellington, 77
Western Engineer (steamboat), 55
Wheat, 38, 41, **48,** 49, 52, 78, 79
White, Mary, 62, 74
White, William Allen, 57, 61, 62, 63, 74
White, William L., 62
White Plume (Chief), **19**
Wichita, 31, 40, 43, 50, 52, 53, 56, 65, 68, 76, **76,** 77, 90
Wichita Indians, 17, 18, 31, 76
Wichita State University, 68
Wichita Symphony, 77
Width, greatest, state, 87
Willard, Jess, 66
Willkie, Wendell, 76
Windbreaks, 43
Windsor Hotel, Garden City, 82
Winfield, 95
Woman mayor, first in U.S., 37
Women's suffrage, 38
Wood, Leonard A., 38
Wood carving, 78
Woodring, Harry H., 61
World War I, 38
World War II, 40, 59, 71
Württemberg, Prince of, 24
Wyandot Indians, 21, 65, 67, 69, 70
Wyandotte, 28, 52, 69
Wyandotte County, 23
Zinc, 43, 55

94

An annual Bluegrass festival is held at Winfield.

PICTURE CREDITS

ABOUT THE AUTHOR

With the publication of his first book for school use when he was twenty, **Allan Carpenter** began a career as an author that has spanned more than 135 books. After teaching in the public schools of Des Moines, Mr. Carpenter began his career as an educational publisher at the age of twenty-one when he founded the magazine *Teachers Digest*. In the field of educational periodicals, he was responsible for many innovations. During his many years in publishing, he has perfected a highly organized approach to handling large volumes of factual material: after extensive traveling and having collected all possible materials, he systematically reviews and organizes everything. From his apartment high in Chicago's John Hancock Building, Allan recalls, "My collection and assimilation of materials on the states and countries began before the publication of my first book." Allan is the founder of Carpenter Publishing House and of Infordata International, Inc., publishers of *Issues in Education* and *Index to U. S. Government Periodicals*. When he is not writing or traveling, his principal avocation is music. He has been the principal bassist of many symphonies, and he managed the country's leading non-professional symphony for twenty-five years.

DATE DUE

FEB 23	MAY 1	6	
MAR 1	MAY 1 3		
MAR 1	MAY 0 6		
JAN 3 1	FEB 20		
MAR1 9			
APR 2			
MAY 1 4			
FEB 0 2			
MAY 0 4			
MAR 3			

C-1

917.81   Carpenter, Allan
CAR   Kansas